T0274897

MASTERS OF TONEWOOD

Masters of Tonewood

The Hidden Art of Fine Stringed-Instrument Making

Jeffrey Greene

UNIVERSITY OF VIRGINIA PRESS
Charlottesville and London

University of Virginia Press
© 2022 by Jeffrey Greene
All rights reserved
Printed in the United States of America on acid-free paper

First published 2022

1 3 5 7 9 8 6 4 2

Library of Congress Cataloging-in-Publication Data

Names: Greene, Jeffrey, author.
Title: Masters of tonewood : the hidden art of fine stringed-instrument making /
Jeffrey Greene.
Description: Charlottesville : University of Virginia Press, 2022. |
Includes bibliographical references and index.
Identifiers: LCCN 2021042951 (print) | LCCN 2021042952 (ebook) |
ISBN 9780813947464 (hardcover) | ISBN 9780813947471 (ebook)
Subjects: LCSH: Stringed instruments—Construction. | Tonewoods. | Forests and forestry.
Classification: LCC ML755 .G82 2022 (print) | LCC ML755 (ebook) | DDC 787/.19—dc23
LC record available at https://lccn.loc.gov/2021042951
LC ebook record available at https://lccn.loc.gov/2021042952

All photographs by the author unless otherwise noted.

Cover art: Violin image, iStock.com/annedehaas; background image,
photo courtesy of Jeffrey Greene/Cremona Musica/30 September 2018

For Mary, and for Roger Raymond

In memory of Mark Harrill Saunders (1966–2019),
director of the University of Virginia Press

And as I wake, sweet music breathe
Above, about, or underneath,
Sent by some Spirit to mortals good,
Or th' unseen Genius of the wood.

—*Il Penseroso*, John Milton

CONTENTS

MASTERS OF TONEWOOD

Tuning Up

AN INTRODUCTION

THE HISTORY OF CHORDOPHONES—stringed instruments—goes back much further than that of their oldest extant artifacts, such as the lyres from 4,500 years ago found in the Mesopotamian royal cemetery at Ur. We know this from images that have outlasted the instruments themselves in ancient archaeological finds. Versions of chordophones emerged in cultures on virtually every habitable continent, and Western musicians today have instruments developed in Asia, the Middle East, and North Africa to thank for the evolution of the modern violin, viola, cello, bass, harp, guitar, and piano. The piano, currently the most popular instrument in the world, evolved from a zither, an early stringed instrument played with sticks. Fundamentally, the piano is a harp strung on a cast-iron frame with a bridge, fitted over a soundboard in an acoustically sensitive piece of furniture. Violins, violas, cellos, and double basses evolved from one of the single- or double-stringed bowed instruments that came to the West via the silk trade.

One of the principal elements that give a distinctive voice to truly great acoustical instruments—a Stradivarius, say, or a Steinway piano—is impeccable tonewood. When luthiers are asked what specific forest produces the wood that makes their instruments sing, they often have not given it much thought, or they generalize, knowing that Italian and Sitka spruce, Balkan maple, and Central American mahogany are prized. They select the finest wood by the way it feels, its weight and flexibility, the quality of its grain, and finally the sound it makes when tapped. They rely on tradition, trusted sources, and years of experience, housing and aging their stock as carefully as others might a collection of the finest wine. Naturally, musicians care deeply about the voice and beauty of their instruments, but they may not be familiar with the forests from which they originate—unless, that is, their instruments contain wood of an endangered species, such as Brazilian rosewood, and they are obliged to register them when transporting them internationally.

I have played various instruments, primarily guitar, from an early age and continue to write lyrics for music decades later. One of my greatest pleasures has been to attend concerts nearly every week, mostly chamber music, in which the instruments themselves are featured for their exquisite sound and history. Instruments possess intrinsic beauty, both in their materials and in forms adapted to the human body. Through discussions with musician and luthier friends and my own keen love of trees, I have begun to understand an important coactive relationship between silviculture—the growing and nurturance of woodlands—in rare mountain forest areas, the art of stringed-instrument making, and the evolution of musical traditions.

Roger Raymond, a French forestry professor who knew of my interests, recommended a book on tonewood, a category that encompasses specific woods used in the making of high-quality stringed instruments. In *Bois de musique: La forêt berceau de l'harmonie,* author Jean-Marie Ballu identifies seven forests in seven European countries that produce some of the world's highest quality tonewood, and because of my interest in both instruments and forests, I felt inspired to visit each of them. Forestry experts manage most of these forests, which are strictly protected by laws; but others still fall prey to commercial logging enterprises that use illegal and harmful cutting practices. Some of the greatest luthiers in Western history are directly associated with these forests, as are prominent instrument-making schools and instrument factories that distribute worldwide.

Over the centuries, the quality of this tonewood has contributed to the perfection of certain stringed instruments, an inspiration of luthiers working in proximity to great forests. In writing this book, I have researched luthiers, tonewood millers, and factory managers in these parts of Europe and set up appointments to meet them. In the course of our conversations, I would learn of other experts or forests to visit. As a result, my project expanded beyond the initial seven countries to include Spain and the United States.

Masters of Tonewood records a journey to some of the historically important centers from which our stringed instruments come. The narrative details the ways in which rare and valuable logs are selected, cut, aged, and processed into billets—blocks of superior wood that, in the hands of master luthiers, are carved into the world's finest stringed

Map of Europe indicating key locations discussed in the book. (Nat Case, INCase, LLC)

instruments. Some of these instruments have elaborate biographies of their own, changing owner multiple times and sometimes traveling from continent to continent over a period of centuries. Each of them has its own distinctive voice, acquired from the characteristics of individual trees, the exigencies of handcrafting, and the generations of musicians who have added tonal depth through their playing. And alas, all of them, however cherished and well cared for, have finite lives. Conversations with foresters, luthiers, musicians, and factory executives in many different countries shed light on the influences and interactions that go into crafting the stringed instruments that provide some of our most pleasurable moments as players and listeners.

1

Origins

DURING HIS EXPERIMENT IN asceticism and living deliberately at Walden, Thoreau famously questioned technological developments as a reliable measure of human progress. He noted, "Our inventions are wont to be pretty toys, which distract us from serious things. They are an improved means to an unimproved end." Choosing the emergence of the telegraph as a particular example, he writes querulously, "We are in great haste to construct a magnetic telegraph from Maine to Texas; but Maine and Texas, it may be, have nothing important to communicate." The telegraph, however, reemerges in a wholly different light in his rhapsodic journal entry of September 22, 1851:

> Yesterday and today the stronger winds of autumn have begun to blow, and the telegraph harp has sounded loudly. I heard it especially in the Deep Cut this afternoon, the tone varying with the tension of different parts of the wire. The sound proceeds from near the posts, where the vibration is apparently more rapid. I put my ear to one of the posts, and it seemed to me as if every pore of the wood was filled with music, labored with the strain—as if every fiber was affected

and being seasoned or timed, rearranged according to a new and more harmonious law. Every swell and change or inflection of tone pervaded and seemed to proceed from the wood, the divine tree or wood, as if its very substance was transmuted. What a recipe for preserving wood, perchance—to keep it from rotting—to fill its pores with music! How this wild tree from the forest, stripped of its bark and set up here, rejoices to transmit this music!

Thoreau's description of the "telegraph harp" effectively summarizes the functioning principles of all stringed instruments: a vibrating wire or string amplified by resonant wood. More significant, the idea of wood fiber from the tree being seasoned and then transmuted by vibration captures the essence of mature tonewood endowed with acoustical brilliance.

A lifelong flute player, Thoreau would likely not dismiss musical instruments as "pretty toys" meant to distract us from life's important meanings. He celebrated the correspondences of nature's songs and the most moving human ones. The master foresters, who have a rare instinct for finding the best tonewood trees, will place an ear against a broad spruce trunk and knock on it to detect "divine" musical potential within. The early autumn winds portend the precise winter moment for cutting.

When musicians, luthiers, and foresters talk about great stringed instruments, they often use rapturous, even anthropomorphic, language that can elevate a telegraph pole to an aeolian harp. A single note from a great Stradivarius can rivet an audience. Violinist Rose Mary Harbinson once commented that the power of a sustained pitch on a Stradivarius "can take the audience by the throat." Cremonese "golden age" instruments of the seventeenth and eighteenth centuries were—and are—known to possess their own personalities. They could project even in a large concert hall. The spruce that voices these personalities reportedly came from trees in the Val di Fiemme, the Paneveggio forest in the Italian Alps that foresters sometimes refer to as "a cathedral of trees."

The violin family of instruments, the piano, and the guitar evolved through a vast if sketchy network of influences from Africa, the Near East, and Asia. However, the refinement of these instruments—at least as Western Europeans understand refinement—occurred most notably in Northern Italy in the sixteenth through eighteenth centuries

Aeolian harp in the Berlin Musical Instrument Museum.

with the famous Cremonese masters Amati, Stradivari, and Guarneri, supported by papal, royal, and aristocratic commissions. Centers for luthiers and instrument making burgeoned in Europe, many associated with specific forest areas that offered rare Norway spruce and figured maple tonewood. Skilled artisans crafted these tonewoods into masterpieces that are still being played by some of the world's most accomplished musicians. Some are on display in museums, where they are also played to maintain their responsiveness while affording audiences an opportunity to hear the individual voices of these instruments.

So where does *your* stringed instrument come from? Thoreau wrote, "Every swell and change or inflection of tone pervaded and seemed to proceed from the wood." Your stringed instrument comes from a forest growing in strictly defined environmental conditions, and luthiers and musicians will tell you the wood is still living, responding to warmth or cold, humidity or dryness, making it at times unruly. For top-quality instruments, even the varnish is an elastic and breathing skin.

How a stringed instrument acquires its unique, even mysterious personality provides a complex story that includes numerous musical traditions, the works of composers and musicians who contribute to those traditions, the inventiveness and innovations of luthiers who strive to perfect an instrument's voice, and finally the foresters who select and cut the music trees. Most important of all are the rare and vanishing forests that produce old trees and the wood that rejoices in transmitting music.

2

A Musical Instrument
Is More than a Tool

IS A MUSICAL INSTRUMENT merely a tool, or does it have a life of its own? Philosophers, writers, and musicians have long argued that tools can enslave us or inspire us. Violinist and conductor Pinchas Zuckerman, however, came to a monistic understanding of his instrument. He once held up his Guarnerius and announced, "To me this is not a tool. Never was. In fact, for me, this is a complete extension of my being."

The greatest musicians gaze at their instruments in wonder, reflecting on the challenges, potential, and sometimes the limitations they present. Even late in their lives, masters such as the cellist Pablo Casals and the guitarist Andrés Segovia would admit there is always progress to be made. The quality or personality of an instrument can enhance or impede the player's progress. For an array of reasons, top musicians commission instruments to be made specifically for themselves. It might be that their eighteenth-century Cremonese instrument is temperamental when on tour, requiring a backup; or a musician may want to explore a customized voice, a tonal coloring that might lead to artistic discoveries.

Sometimes, playability and response become critical. This was the case for the British cello virtuoso Jacqueline du Pré, who during her mercurial career owned and played two Stradivarius cellos, one made in 1681 and the other her beloved "Davidov." All of du Pré's recordings between 1965 and 1968 featured the latter Stradivarius. She also played for two years on a cello made by Matteo Goffriller, another Italian master luthier of the seventeenth and eighteenth centuries appreciated for his cellos. When celebrated musicians and conductors discuss du Pré's gifts, three qualities invariably emerge: her complete mastery of the cello, her capacity for absorbing and internalizing music almost instantly, and her ability to elevate all who worked with her; she is often described as a powerful instrumental conversationalist. Charles Beare, a leading expert on stringed instruments who worked with du Pré, recalled how she tested a new instrument: "I remember vividly her way of trying out a cello was to play a note fairly low down on the D string. She played that note for two or three minutes, and you wouldn't believe the variety of sound and volume and beauty she could get out of it."

Beare spoke on other occasions of du Pré's brilliant playing of an F on a D string: "You lost all sense of time, and she got more into that note . . . than most people can get into a concerto." Beare added that du Pré would instinctively devise her own approaches to Schumann, for example, that the composer himself might have wished he had thought of. Tragically, with the onset of multiple sclerosis, belatedly diagnosed, she experienced difficulties controlling her cello playing. Her confidence and sincerity were undermined, replaced by self-consciousness and ultimately the need to follow fingering by eye. Biographer Carol Easton writes that "the combination of her forceful playing and the hypersensitivity of her cellos necessitated frequent adjustments and caused her considerable anxiety, particularly in a large hall. She worried that her sound might not carry above the orchestra, or that the cello would get—her expressions—a terrible 'wolf note' or 'buzz,' or start 'kicking' or 'bubbling.'"

Daniel Barenboim, du Pré's husband and musical soulmate, commissioned Italian American Sergio Peresson, considered by many to be the greatest twentieth-century luthier, to make a cello specifically for her. The new cello provided the volume, stability, and "quick and easy" response that du Pré desperately needed during what turned out to be the close of her career at age twenty-eight. Her last three performances were the Brahms Double Concerto with Pinchas Zukerman and the New York Philharmonic conducted by Leonard Bernstein. A fourth concert was scheduled, but du Pré could not even feel the weight of her bow, leaving her shattered. A new program had to be substituted, with Isaac Stern playing.

When I am in the presence of professional cellists and du Pré's name comes up, the tone automatically shifts to reverence. In a sunny kitchen in the heart of Paris, I spoke to Henri Alécian about commissioning a luthier to construct a new cello, and he hardly paused over my raising the question of du Pré needing the Peresson instrument. "She was exceptional in her intensity, possessed impeccable musicality and sincerity. She had a tragic destiny." For du Pré, a new cello became part of that destiny. Henri recalled a far less dramatic case of an esteemed musician turning to a modern instrument: the great French cellist André Navarra, who played an eighteenth-century cello made by the Neapolitan luthier Nicolò Gagliano. Though the Gagliano cello was an extremely fine and valuable cello, Navarra at the end of his career preferred a modern cello, made by a relatively unknown luthier, that was not nearly as beautiful but was still very effective, with a great sound.

Because of a desire to achieve a strong voice and to overcome the shortcomings of his own instrument, Alécian was motivated to acquire a new cello. "I worked with a little cello made around 1740, very pretty, a baroque instrument made by Jacob Rauch, luthier for the court in Mannheim. I found it very capricious and difficult to play, yet it had a lovely sound. It required constant adjustments for its baroque set-up." Alécian got up from the table and fetched the cello, which was indeed handsome and was undoubtedly still a valuable instrument. The body was a nearly uniform natural blond color, with a spruce top but maple back and sides without the typical vivid maple figuring. The varnish having worn off added to the light natural color. Alécian explained, "Often the older instruments like this are wonderful, but sometimes they can be unreliable because the wood is old. It might be more sensitive to changes in humidity or temperature. A baroque instrument with gut strings can go out of tune every five minutes, which is maddening during concerts. But then again, well-made modern instruments can experience variations too."

After years of researching and trying out cellos, Alécian finally commissioned one. "I had heard of the luthier Prochasson from other professional cellists," he told me. "He had made instruments for soloists Philippe Muller and Emmanuelle Bertrand, among others. I went to the Salon Musicora for maybe ten years when the event was still very good and had many top exhibitors. I tried different cellos while looking for a luthier. I especially liked Prochasson's instruments and each year would return to admire his work."

"When I finally ordered one," Alécian continued, "Prochasson explained that it would take two years to make. He asked what style of instrument most interested me—Guarneri, Montagnana, Goffriller, or Stradivari. I told him that I wanted a very classic cello because during that era the master luthiers were great experimenters who ultimately refined the quartet instruments. A cello based on a Strad would suit me perfectly. At the time, he wanted to work on a model derived from the Cristiani. The Cristiani is very, very big, and for his version he slightly reduced the dimensions."

I knew in advance that Prochasson had modeled the new cello on the Stradivarius Stauffer ex Cristiani 1700, the jewel of the Museo del Violino collection in Cremona. The Consorzio Liutai Antonio Stradivari Cremona produced a stunning—and enormous—book detailing the history of the instrument, along with all its technical data, including the chemical makeup of the wood and the stain and varnish, optical daylight and UV light examinations, and an analysis of every miniscule particle, fissure, and crater. Maps of thicknesses, repairs, and patterns of wear were included in the volume as well, along with a full-size poster of the instrument.

Alécian was enamored of the book when I showed it to him. He brought out his cello to compare with the recorded specifications. He noted that the wood grain in both cello tops was broad, an important detail that Prochasson matched. Alécian ran a tape measure lengthwise and confirmed that the body of his cello was indeed one-third of an inch shorter, but the other dimensions were the same. "It's very close," he observed. This meant that Alécian was playing a large cello in contrast to his little one. As Harry Mairson, who used computed tomography to scan the Cristiani, wrote, "It's really too big for a modern musician to play—roughly 2 centimeters [0.8 inches] longer than the modern standard. Violoncellos, originally used to play simple bass lines in church music, later became virtuoso instruments. Their size consequently decreased, giving the player access to more positions on the fingerboard. Pitch standards changed. And string technology improved." Many early Stradivarius cellos were taken apart and cut down in size during the late eighteenth century. Size did not seem to impede Alécian, however. With the sun beaming through the kitchen windows, he held his cello above the poster and smiled at the comparison.

Like a copy painter in the Louvre, Prochasson had even reproduced with staining the patterns of wear, but the color was different: the Cristiani appeared more plum-tinted. Alécian said, "I didn't really understand color. I said to him, 'Not too dark, reddish, or orangish,' but I didn't expect it to turn out to be so light. But it was too late." He laughed. "*Voila*. This is a very good cello, but, as you know, there is always an instrument better or different. In my case, I like this cello very much, and I am likely to work with it always. On occasion, I have played an exceptional instrument, above all an Italian instrument from the eighteenth century. Some are not fully identified, but still I knew when it was extraordinary."

Nine years earlier, on a summer evening at the École de musique de Buc, I had watched Alécian perform in the Trio Hadaly as the late sunlight angled from the concert hall window onto his new cello, which so closely resembled the Cremona masterpiece. The incarnation of the Stauffer ex Cristiani 1700 was so newly born that the varnish appeared to be still tacky. Alécian's playing was radiant, the outpouring of a musician, each heightening the other's potential. Musicians and luthiers speak of "opening up" a new instrument, meaning that playing it literally improves its sound.

Jean-Louis Prochasson's workshop is located in the Loire Valley city of Tours, where he shares space with church sculpture restoration experts. When he led me to the entrance of his workshop, we passed carvings of angels and saints centuries old and in need of cleaning, along with newly carved replacement parts and paint touchups. Like many luthiers, Prochasson had hung life-size images of great violins, violas, and cellos about his shop, images so accurate that he could use them directly as models for measurements. Prochasson owned the same book on the Stauffer ex Cristiani 1700 that I had (again) brought with me. Carefully researching masterpieces fit Prochasson's planning method. Discussing Alécian's cello, he commented, "The Cristiani was a Stradivarius model that I found very beautiful. Others seemed narrow, but this instrument was very large. In fact, it's the largest Strad that we know. The year I decided to make this instrument, this detailed book on the Cristiani had been published. It was destiny, as this book helped me. I had the opportunity to listen to the Cristiani in a trio concert when I was in Cremona for the Mondomusica. It possesses superb deep tones."

Prochasson had followed an unconventional path to becoming a luthier. He studied graphic design in Paris, but after graduating spent years learning his craft in Cremona, where he could examine some of the most famous Italian instruments. He also developed an unusual interest in using spruce with wider grain than is often seen in the tops of instruments. Wisdom holds that tighter grain transmits sound waves more efficiently, but Prochasson explored the range of sound qualities using different grains. A wider grain is one of the distinguishing features of the Cristiani cello, and he managed to replicate it with impressive accuracy.

"I like large grain like this, above all for the cello. On the last one I made, the grain was quite wide." Prochasson showed a piece of wood left over from the new cello belly, and the grain was indeed even wider than on his Cristiani model. "The grain is very wide all the way to the end, but the wood is light and I made the vault much higher. I hope this makes the instrument warmer. But we apply human sensibilities, and you can't accurately predict the sound you will get just from the grain."

Prochasson is the type of luthier who focuses on custom work according to a musician's wishes, so he maintains a broad spectrum of tonewoods in his stock. He picks and chooses rather than taking many billets from a single tree, which had been the case with some of the Stradivarius instruments. Scientists have genetically verified through samples from instruments that Stradivari would exploit a single log.

Alécian's cello has assumed a life of its own through its responsiveness, resonance, and range, an identity that concert programs can extol. Often, for chamber music concerts, an instrument will have its biography printed along with the musician's. In the case of Alécian's cello, the audience can expect acoustical qualities similar to those of the Stauffer ex Cristiani 1700. The name derives, in part, from the Fondazione Walter Stauffer, which donated the Stradivarius cello to the city of Cremona and its Strings Collection. The instrument had once belonged to one of history's most extraordinary cellists, the Parisian Elise Barbier Cristiani, who owned her namesake Stradivarius only briefly owing to her tragically short life. In 1856, Lise Cristiani, the first professional female cellist, died at age twenty-five of cholera in Siberia. Her Stradivarius bears not only her name but also her physical impression in the wood itself, the maturation of which was in part a response to her playing of the instrument. Here was a woman who not only played the cello when it was deemed unfeminine but also performed publicly with the instrument cradled scandalously between her knees instead of being held sidesaddle fashion. Despite Harry Mairson's comment that the cello was too large for the modern player, Lise Cristiani seemed to have managed the giant cello perfectly well. In fact, judging from reviews of her concerts, music scholars surmise that she was particularly gifted at high notes on an instrument appreciated for its "superb deep notes."

In the mid-nineteenth century, she performed in major cities throughout Europe. On hearing a performance, Mendelssohn was inspired to compose one of his famous Lieder ohne Worte (Songs without Words) for piano, Opus 109, which he dedicated to Cristiani. She also toured the world, playing even in parts of eastern Russia, where audiences had never heard a cello before. Reporting in a letter to her family in Paris an encounter with a whale while crossing the Sea of Okhotsk, she proposed fancifully that the animal might have been drawn to the voice of her Stradivarius:

> We did not see it again until the day came, when it waved its tail
> in the air a mile from us. As the Stradivari had serenaded the wind
> and the waves with its sweetest tunes the previous evening, we
> thought that the cetacean might have been attracted. A naturalist
> accompanying us did not say no, and from that moment the general
> opinion on board was that whales, like turtles, must be first class
> music lovers.

No one would consider a custom-built stringed instrument a novelty, given the number of luthiers still crafting them, but nowadays factories produce very good instruments, and one can easily imagine the competitive strain on the artisans. Magali Barthe, who runs a shop specializing in bows on the rue de Rome in Paris, put the problem in perspective: "Today, 90 percent of the violins for children come from China and Korea for a sales price in France of $500. No French luthier could produce and sell a new violin for a child for less than $3,000."

The cello that Jean-Louis Prochasson built for Alécian pays tribute to the acoustical innovation and craft of the golden age Cremonese master luthiers and their families: Andrea Amati and sons Gerolamo and Antonio, Giuseppe Guarneri and son Giuseppe Guarneri del Gesù, Carlo Bergonzi and sons Michele Angelow and Zosimo, and Antoine Stradivari and sons Francesco and Omobono. These masters refined the violin, viola, and cello to such a degree that hardly anyone since has significantly improved on them. It is the enduring public passion for the artistic tradition and the music produced by these great instruments that keeps them—and the artisans who produce them—alive.

Interactions of composers, musicians, and luthiers inspire instrumental music. Mendelssohn was moved to compose one of his numerous Songs without Words for piano after hearing Lise Cristiani passionately playing her Stradivarius. Her instrument, in turn, was made in Cremona and bought in Paris from Auguste Sébastien Philippe Bernardel, a gifted luthier and a key figure in preserving the great Cremonese instruments that had made their way to France. Many of these instruments were rescued from outright neglect in Italian noble houses and monasteries by a mercurial carpenter and violin dealer named Luigi Tarisio. Cellist Christian Bellisario captures the spectrum of feelings evoked by holding and playing a Stradivarius: "The whole range of human emotions and desires [is] brought into play, from the higher feelings to baser sentiments, from wonder, admiration, contemplation and joy to covetousness, fetishism and opportunism."

But there is another element of Stradivarius magic, too: the story of rare woods, carefully chosen, milled, and aged to produce an exceptional instrument that can spellbind audiences with its curves and warm colors and evoke through its voice a vast range of human emotions.

Where do you begin if you want an excellent instrument? Ask a salesperson? Research the higher-quality Chinese and Korean instruments and try them? Or do you go to the best New York, London, Cremona, and

Paris luthiers? Do you commission a bespoke instrument or purchase one that has a history and has matured and acquired a voice?

The professional cellist Sarah Hammel Gueta started higher studies at the Royal Academy of Music in London, where she worked with an eighteenth-century cello that the school's museum lent her. Then, as a gift, her parents commissioned a cello to be made for her by Patrick Robin as she was about to pursue graduate studies at the Yale School of Music. Robin, whose workshop is in Angers, had garnered a hoard of gold medals for his violins, violas, and cellos, and internationally recognized soloists were playing them. Luthiers such as Robin, along with Andrea Frandsen and Jacques Bauer, have put Angers on the map as a center for some of the very best instrument making in Europe. In all such workshops, protégés who have already attended luthier schools spend additional apprenticeship years absorbing and mastering the techniques and skills while freeing their imaginations to consider innovations that might give their instruments a signature sound.

Hammel Gueta's instrument came from Patrick Robin's workshop and was made under the master's supervision; but apprentice Antoine Cauche crafted it and maintained it. Years later, when Hammel Gueta was a music professor herself, she would share her cello, passing the gorgeous instrument back and forth, professor to students. The experience provided a perfect introduction to a high-quality instrument. I asked her what it was like playing a newly created cello.

"Being the first one to play an instrument is always an extremely important moment," Sarah responded. "You give a second life to the wood. It's a moment of rebirth. It develops a new life, a musical life. The difference between playing an old instrument versus a new instrument is very substantial. For an old instrument, you can feel the history of the instrument having been played by many other musicians. It has a story already. With the new instrument, you are the one giving the vibration to the wood; you are forming it in relation to what you want to hear. You are in a way much closer to nature, closer to the essence of the materials you are using. It is a privileged experience. I like to compare it to the life of a human being: by playing young wood it's as if you help it grow old in a beautiful way."

Angers, not far from Prochasson in Tours, is one of the most attractive of the Loire Valley cities, with a history of supporting the arts since the Middle Ages. That spirit of arts patronage still exists, and luthiers benefit from it. The striking château d'Angers, built in bands of bone-colored limestone and dark schist, features the Apocalypse Tapestry, commissioned by the Duke of Anjou in the fourteenth century. Medieval imagery in some panels shows angels playing various instruments, including an early version of a violin. Images like these allow musicologists to understand the origins of instruments whose predecessors long ago disappeared, having been made of ephemeral organic materials.

Hammel Gueta's luthier, Antoine Cauche, was named Chevalier de l'Ordre des Arts et des Lettres for his contributions to the art of lutherie in France. Like Patrick Robin, he has won international gold medals for string quartet instruments, including one for a viola on display in the Museo del Violino in Cremona, along with the Cristiani. Cauche is a thin, handsome man with a trim beard, younger than one would expect for someone with such an impressive trove of accomplishments. He works in a space that looks like a cross between a surgery unit and a furniture maker's shop where wood billets age, exhibiting the traced outlines of instrument backs and tops. All around are bottles of oil, resins, pigments, and varnish elixirs. For anyone who loves the odor of wood and varnish, this space is an opium den. On my visit, the violin, viola, and cello molds for wrapping and gluing the curved maple sides were lined up on a shelf, some with joints braced and drying. Cauche's workroom appeared meticulously clean except for the curls of microplaned wood decorating spaces on the main workbench and forming a neat pile on the wooden floor. The craft tools were hung

Antoine Cauche, luthier, holding a form used for making the sides of a cello, in his workshop near Angers, France.

in custom-made wooden cribs and slots on the wall: chisels, files, calipers, braces, saws, mallets, rulers, clamps, and planes. A violin and a viola hung next to a supply of maple bridges.

A sibling to Hammel Gueta's instrument had just been finished and tested in preparation for Cauche's final adjustments, which might include positioning the sound post (called *anima* in Italian or *ame* in French, both meaning "soul"), a seemingly innocuous dowel that runs between the front and back plates in the instrument's body. Interestingly, adding the sound post was a major resonance innovation introduced by the great Italian luthiers, many crediting Amati. Most of the quartet instruments have four strings, although some baroque instruments feature one or two more. Modern strings are made of steel, sometimes steel wound around silk or sheep-gut. The bow, which consists of a carefully carved stick, holds taut strands of horsehair that

A cello in the making in Antoine Cauche's workshop near Angers, France.

are rubbed with rosin to increase friction. When the musician draws the bow across the strings, sound vibrations are transmitted through the bridge to the instrument's belly plate. The innovation of the sound post allows the belly vibration to pass efficiently to the back plate, further amplifying the sound projected forward through the f-holes.

Cauche played the new instrument aggressively in a pleasing way, but it was not a recognizable piece of music. "This is what luthiers do," he said. "We play a bunch of notes to hear what we made." Growing up in Toulouse, Cauche loved both music and working with wood, but he did not formally pursue his passion for lutherie until after he had graduated from the lycée, the French equivalent of high school. In France and in other European countries, lutherie training begins in high school, and having few formal options in France to pursue instrument making, Cauche opted to enroll in the International School of Newark in England, which has an outstanding program in musical instrument crafts. Cauche would go on to apprentice for eight years with Patrick Robin and Andrea Frandsen, both of whom also studied violin making in Newark but a decade earlier. Setting out on his own, Cauche intended to concentrate on making violins, considering them more cost- and time-efficient, but to his surprise, the majority of orders were for his cellos.

Yet another sibling of Hammel Gueta's cello lay in the works, its major elements finished. Cauche placed the top, known as the belly, on his bench and explained that it was made of two billets cut radially from the inner section of a chosen spruce log. The cut is critical if the grain is to form a mirror image when the billets are opened like a book. Cauche ran his finger across the grain. "Do you see how fine these lines are, the growth rings?" he asked. "This gives the wood its resonance. This wood comes from Italy—*Picea* [spruce], like the Cremonese instruments. It has been aged for ten years already, and comes from very old trees from particular altitudes, soil, and disposition to the sun. I have reliable suppliers; and I just tap the wood to test it. It shouldn't make a 'clank' sound at all but a sharp 'click.'"

Cauche picked up a billet leaning next to a counter. "Listen to it. The best tonewood should sound like a Ping-Pong ball, with a sharp clarity." He tapped it a few times with his fingernail. "Hear that? That's rare." He turned the billet back and forth. "No imperfections," he observed appreciatively. Cauche's mentor Patrick Robin once told him, "Spruce is like mountain people, light and strong. The higher the altitude, the lighter and stronger they get."

Cauche works almost exclusively with spruce and maple for the quartet instruments. "It's traditional," he remarked. "Musicians shun any variations."

Hardly any tonewood can match a tight-grained spruce top for quartet instruments. The top provides the voice. Choice spruce from high altitudes is light but rigid, with excellent acoustical properties that only improve with time. Flamed or tiger maple is another excellent tonewood, one that is also highly appreciated for its aesthetic appeal. For reasons that are neither entirely understood nor detectable from the outside of an individual tree, the sycamore maple—and many other trees—can develop an undulating growth pattern that affects the grain of the wood, producing a seemingly three-dimensional figuring. A number of evocative terms are used to describe figuring: flame, quilted, ghost, crotched, bear claw, bird's eye, and dimpled. Each has its own pattern. While flamed maple is traditional for the instruments of the violin family, guitar makers use a wide variety of figured woods, including rosewood and koa.

If you look carefully at the back and sides of a good violin, viola, or cello, you can get the impression that you are seeing a hologram. This effect is called *chatoyancy,* a French term derived from *chat* (cat) and *oeil* (eye) and generally used to describe the appearance of such gemstones as chrysoberyl, moonstones, and tourmaline. Tiger's eye quartz resembles most closely the striped, honeyed iridescence of stained flamed maple. Almost any guitar enthusiast would recognize Gibson's traditional flame-top Les Paul. Clients can order one from the Gibson factory with an A, AA, or AAA top, paying progressively more along the way for the added workmanship and the fine definition of the tigerlike stripes.

Cauche's instrument lay in the throes of its creation, and here were its parts: the elegant arched top, the lines of purfling along the edge, the simple, clean f-holes. The luthier picked up the top and turned it over, pointing out that it had been carved at the end with finger planes. Penciled numbers looked like a nautical depth chart in a bay.

Cauche demonstrated a rather large caliper that could precisely measure the thickness of the carved parts of a cello. "I gave this top more of an arch because the density of the wood demanded more volume," he explained. He retrieved the form for a cello around which the sides were already wrapped, the glue still drying. The curved wood met at the corners of C-shaped cuts at the waist, where the bow passes. The side pieces were flamed maple, strips that were molded and glued to spruce corner blocks. The back, like the front, was carved from matching billets, but this time they too were of flamed maple. The sides had matching maple from the same log, which probably had come from Eastern Europe, Romania, or Bosnia-Herzegovina.

The purfling inlay on the back had also been finished. Purfling looks like simple outline decoration, but it serves an important purpose. Made from soft wood, the inlay absorbs expansion and contraction of the wood with changing weather conditions and humidity, as well as offering protection from shocks. These changes can result in cracks and splitting at the edges of the fronts and backs. Without purfling, the cracks can travel along the grain through the plates. Again, Andrea Amati is credited with this innovation, which was quickly adopted and later made more elaborately decorative for use on guitars and other instruments. The crafting and style of the purfling became a luthier's signature and one of the standards by which a skillfully made instrument is judged. Ordinarily, a fine groove is meticulously chiseled at the perimeter of the fronts and backs. The purfling itself consists of a very thin, three-ply lamination. Italian luthiers originally used dyed pearwood, sometimes black and white, to give a decorative highlight.

The neck, made from a single block of flamed maple, remained the least finished part, yet its noble scroll head was already fully carved, as was the tuning box, cleanly drilled with holes for the pegs. Even final preparations for the pitch of the neck—its all-important angle—seemed to be under way. The nut guide for the strings and the ebony fingerboard would follow, along with the final carving and smoothing. Ebony would also be used for the tuning pegs and the tailpiece, which holds the strings at the bottom of the instrument. Violins and violas often have ebony chinrests, and while the use of spruce and maple is standard for the bodies and necks of quartet instruments, tuning pegs also can be made of rosewood, which contains a natural resin that helps prevent slippage. The tailpiece and the chinrests usually match the tuning pegs.

These parts eventually are attached using hoof-and-hide glue, which contains properties essential for lutherie. It shrinks to tighten joints and is weak enough to give under stress before the wood does, reducing damage. It also allows an instrument to be readily opened if repairs are required. The glue spoils on the shelf, so it comes in granules to be prepared as needed.

Cauche must know from long experience how transforming it is for musicians to see their instruments under construction, inside and out. The process provides a sense of intimacy. Cauche put the body on display for a client to convey a sense of what the finished instrument would look like (although the spruce grain and wavy patterns in flamed maple would be far more evident after the stain and varnish were applied). The pale body parts looked ghostly.

While the varnish protects the wood from dirt, grease, and sweat, it also contributes to both aesthetics and sound. The transparency and the tint of the varnish make the finest details of the spruce and maple grain structure much more vivid, similar to polishing agate. In terms of sound, the very best varnishes remain elastic; they respire with the wood and allow it to vibrate freely. Experts have compared violin varnish to skin, a key part of the evolving life of the instrument.

Cauche also explained that the varnish can temper too much brightness in the voice.

The dark-honey varnishes made of resins and oil give Cauche's stringed instruments an autumnal look. On the newly finished cello, the layers of varnish seemed to magnify the spruce grain and imbue the flamed maple back and sides with an iridescent, almost three-dimensional effect. The key to obtaining this look in figured maple is to apply primary ground coating to the newly finished cello to seal the wood fibers and prevent deep varnish penetration. The Brooklyn luthier Sam Zygmuntowicz compared applying ground to a painter's application of a preparatory layer of gesso to a canvas before painting on it. Some believe that the ground, for which numerous formulas exist, is a critical component of the instrument's sound, reasoning that varnish on a Stradivarius is often thin—if not worn off completely—and yet the instrument retains its cherished sound. Most experts are detractors. Still, Stradivari was known to use a solution comprising quartz, calcite, feldspar, and gypsum. Different ground recipes abound, some featuring oils, propolis, casein, or eggs.

While the sibling cello looked like a twin of Sarah's instrument, Cauche emphasized that every handmade instrument is different. It might be based on the designs of a seventeenth- or eighteenth-century master and closely resemble other works by the same luthier, but it still has its own sound and feel. Cauche explained some of the adjustments he made to give this cello its particular resonance. Most significant was the deeper vault he created in its belly, not because of the wider grain as Prochasson had done (this top had tight grain) but because he perceived the wood was a little soft and needed more size for vibration.

Good luthiers have professional musicians test their new instruments. For this particular cello, the musician was so pleased that he used it on a recording. It was at this point that Cauche told me that a new instrument would acquire a voice, that it needed to be opened up by being played rigorously and for years. Some musicians who play the great Italian instruments become superstitious about this, about what faults might develop. The Cristiani instrument, for example, had minute cracks from the time Lise played with a whale hugging the hull of her ship in the Sea of Okhotsk, when she performed for Tolstoy and across Russia. When one of his newly made instruments comes back to Cauche for maintenance, he can hear the maturing process. "The difference is often profound," he asserted. The cello is a kind of evolving creature constructed of rare organic materials, and here it was in its living skin.

3

Norway Spruce and Figured Maple in Violin Family Instruments

SOME INSTRUMENTS ACQUIRE SUCH a mystique that anthropomorphizing them becomes irresistible. This is often seen in popular music with the pet names famous contemporary musicians give their guitars, such as B. B. King's Lucille (several generations of her) and Keith Richards's Micawber. Few instruments, however, can match the charisma of the Cremonese golden era violins, violas, and cellos, in part because they have already survived more than three hundred years and outlived generations of virtuosos, collectors, and benefactors. Sometimes they experience remarkable adventures of neglect and rediscovery. The Stradivarius "Red Mendelssohn" inspired the award-winning film *The Red Violin*. The owner of the Stradivarius, the American solo violinist Elizabeth Pitcairn, remarked, "It's kind of spooky. When I'm playing that Chaconne [by John Corigliano], that's when the violin can tell its own story; that's when it can actually speak."

The fact that the old Cremonese instruments can sell for millions of dollars adds considerably to their mystique. For example, when the "Macdonald" Stradivarius viola was offered at auction, bidding opened at $45 million. A viola is not often considered a solo instrument, even if it does have one of the most human singing voices of all instruments. The "Duport" Stradivarius cello sold for $20 million, the "Vieuxtemps" Guarnerius violin for $16 million.

Many of these cherished instruments have been stolen, some more than once, and a number have never reappeared. They attract intrigues and fraud schemes. One of the more notorious of the latter involved the German instrument dealer Dietmar Machold, who swindled clients out of tens of millions of dollars with fake Stradivarius violins. He was arrested in 2011 and successfully prosecuted.

Then there are extraordinary episodes such as an incident that occurred in 1967, when the violinist David Margetts lost the 1732 Stradivarius "Duke of Alcantara," which he had borrowed while he was second violinist with a University of California, Los Angeles, quartet. Who knows what happened to it? He might have left it on his car roof. Nadia Tupica, a Spanish teacher, discovered a double violin case near a freeway off-ramp. She did not realize that she was in possession of a Stradivarius along with a violin of lesser value. The prized instrument was passed down to family members until a San Francisco luthier who maintained the instrument decided to research it and ultimately uncovered its identity. The reappearance of the violin twenty-seven years later set off an ownership dispute, UCLA versus "finders keepers." In another incident, unlucky virtuoso David Garrett tripped at the end of a concert at London's Barbican Center in 2008 and fell down a step. He landed on the case containing the 1718 Stradivarius "San Lorenzo." When Garrett opened the case, the violin was in pieces. Even the great cellist Yo-Yo Ma suffered a heart-stopping bout of absent-mindedness when he forgot his 1733 Domenico Montagnana "Petunia" in the trunk of a New York City taxicab. A Queens cab driver, the New York City Police Department, and admirers ceremoniously returned the rescued cello to the relieved and grateful owner.

Instruments' sobriquets can be lovely, too. One owner named his 1714 Stradivarius the "Dolphino" because its back reminded him of that elegant aquatic creature. Some experts regard the Dolphino as one of

Stradivari's top three violins, and Jascha Heifetz, sometimes called the world's greatest violinist, once owned and performed with it.

But many of the nicknames are chosen to honor past owners and musicians. Heifetz also owned the "Piel-Heifetz." The Nippon Music Foundation, which purchased the Dolphino, along with eighteen other Stradivarius instruments and two violins made by Guarneri del Gesù, currently owns the Paganini Quartet, named after the great musician and composer. Paganini once possessed the four instruments: the 1727 "Comte Cozio di Salabue" and 1680 "Desaint" violins, the 1731 "Mendelssohn" viola, and perhaps Stradivari's last cello, the 1736 "Ladenburg."

The Nippon Music Foundation is known to have a voracious appetite for acquiring great Cremonese violins, violas, and cellos; but it has also been exceptionally generous in maintaining and lending them to internationally acclaimed musicians and quartets in the cause of promoting classical music. Who wouldn't want to experience a concert with the Paganini Quartet instruments, all made by the same genius?

Joseph Silverstein, a violinist and conductor who played a Guarneri del Gesù, once commented ruefully, "Unfortunately for the modern violinist, we are dealing with a collectable commodity." He understood that a violin made by a Cremonese master, in good condition and with a fine sound, will have three values: one for the collector, one for the player because of its tonal potential, and one for an investor. Silverstein went on to say, "It's very frustrating for me sometimes [when I am] working with a student that I know is a very gifted young player and that student is playing on an instrument that has very distinct limitations. . . . I hope that we will begin to develop modern instruments . . . of sufficient quality that they can grow with it and it can grow with them."

The great appreciation *always finds its way back to the masters,* the ones who set the standard and created the tradition, along with the musicians and composers whose work made them unforgettable. However, some new instruments may already equal those made by

Amati, Stradivari, Guarneri, Bergonzi, Stainer, and the French and German luthiers who followed. Blind tests have been conducted in which both experimenters and listeners were unable to discern distinct differences in the sound quality of old masterpieces and some of the new instruments. Musical acoustics expert Claudia Fritz and luthier Joseph Curtin conducted a double-blind study at Pierre and Marie Curie University in Paris in which ten top violinists listened to and compared modern instruments with venerable old ones—and preferred the modern violins. Still, reverence for the old instruments is stronger now than ever. Richness and authenticity are restored to them when they are fitted with gut strings to replicate the tonality of the original compositions.

An understanding of the acoustical properties of spruce probably dates back to ancient times. The refinement of the violin family of instruments came not from Renaissance science but instead from the direct experiences of woodworkers and the knowledge passed down from master to apprentice, informed by the appreciation of musicians and their patrons. Science can no more explain the extreme musicality of a Stradivarius than it can explain the nuanced flavors of a bottle of rare wine selling for a comparably astronomical price. Psychologists have said we create value through emotions, which also happen to be the key component in music.

Legend has it that Antonio Stradivari would travel the 150 miles north from Cremona to the Paneveggio forest in a section of the alpine range bordering Austria. During the waning winter moon, Stradivari would go out with a hammer and tap on the oldest spruce trees to evaluate their acoustical power. The most exceptional of these would then be sacrificed to the construction of his greatest violins, violas, and cellos.

One can imagine a pilgrimage for Stradivari that would follow the Adige river, skirting Verona to the east and Lake Garda to the west, up to the pink Dolomite mountains and the Paneveggio forest. Even at the end of the seventeenth century, the old-growth trees were not untouched, reflecting the ever-increasing demand for wood. For centuries, even while it was controlled and protected by the aristocracy, the Paneveggio had been a major area for culling timber. Perhaps the great master luthiers *did* make the journey to choose the trees themselves, but little is known about those who supplied and later milled them. The logs were dragged by oxen to the rivers that would carry them to mills near major towns. Part of the curing process occurred in the river water. Three hundred years later, on the path through the Paneveggio violin forest park, visitors will encounter a little exhibit comprised of two logs and a mallet. Children and adults alike are invited to play the role of Stradivari, tapping the logs to hear for themselves the remarkable tones lent by Paneveggio spruce to instruments that would one day sell for $20 million.

Anyone who lives close to trees knows they are noisy beings. One becomes attuned to the changes of weather and seasons announced by the sounds of trees: the new spring leaf rustle, the dry tick of autumn leaf fall, the murmuring and creaking of swaying trunks, the turbulent rushing sound of storm gusts, and the split and crash of branches, sometimes whole trees, in ice storms. Many of us know the knocking and clacking sounds made by unloading and stacking firewood or planks of lumber. While walking in the woods, children might whack trees with a stick for a satisfying sound: indeed, two pieces of wood tapped or clicked together can constitute a musical instrument. In *The Hidden Life of Trees,* Peter Wohlleben describes wood as an efficient transmitter of sound:

> Wood fibers conduct sound particularly well, which is why they are used to make musical instruments such as violins and guitars. You can do a simple experiment to test for yourself how well these acoustics work. Put your ear up against the narrow end of a long trunk on the forest floor and ask another person at the thicker end to carefully make a small knocking or scratching sound with a pebble. On a still day, you can hear the sound through the trunk clearly, even if you lift your head. Birds use this property as an alarm system for their nesting cavities.

When luthier Antoine Cauche explained that tapping on the best Norway spruce billets for violin, viola, or cello tops should elicit the sound of a Ping-Pong ball being struck, he was referring to *sound velocity,* a measurable acoustical property that the best tonewood exhibits. High sound velocity is desirable not only for the bowed quartet instruments but also for piano soundboards, guitar tops, and the bellies of many other instruments. Ordinarily the speed of sound through dry air at a moderate temperature is 1,125 feet per second. Top-level tonewoods can carry sound at a much higher velocity longitudinally along the grain. The sound velocity for Norway spruce can range between 16,000 and 19,500 feet per second, and maple can run between 13,000 to 16,000 feet per second. Higher sound velocity provides greater clarity, sustain, and harmonic range. Other acoustical properties of spruce govern sound duration, timbre, and volume. Norway spruce performs at an exceptionally high level in comparative acoustical testing with other spruce species. That is not to dismiss other instrument woods, which offer their own appreciated tones for guitar tops, mandolins, and pianos.

Norway spruce, *Picea abies,* is one of the most common trees in the Northern Hemisphere. Its native habitat extends from the eastern border of France to the Ural mountain range dividing Europe from Asia. The spruce's range also extends north into the Scandinavian peninsula. Though they particularly thrive in mountainous regions, spruce can also live at near sea level as long as they have enough rain and the summer temperatures remain moderate. The most famous Norway spruce is a thousand-year-old specimen in Sweden named Old Tjikko. After carbon dating its roots, Leif Kullman, professor of physical geography at Umeå University, named the tree after his beloved dog.

Though non-native, Norway spruce has been widely planted throughout the United States and Canada. Every year, Americans enjoy the lighting of the Rockefeller Center Christmas tree, a ceremony that has taken place annually since 1933 and includes broadcasts and staged entertainment. The tree selected is often a towering Norway spruce that, given its size, has probably been around for a while (though spruce grows rapidly in some environments and very slowly in others).

Norway spruce is fairly easy to identify. Its dark green, pendulous branches swoop gracefully upward at their ends, except during the time of year when they are weighed down with a mass of chestnut-colored cones four to eight inches long. The branches flex easily, allowing them to dump a burden of accumulated snow. The one-inch needles hang downward on smaller branches and twigs. The scalelike bark is mottled brown and gray.

While Norway spruce is common, only old individual trees growing under perfect conditions provided tonewood for the violin bellies made by Amati, Stradivari, and Guarneri. Given their own space, spruce trees project broad branches from the base and ever-shorter ones higher up, creating a conical shape. Trees in close proximity to one another can thrive together in an embrace, shading out other species. Norway spruce often grows in particularly tight groves at higher altitudes. The upper canopy allows limited light below, which in turn inhibits the growth of lower limbs. For clean tonewood, the lower trunks of trees must be straight-grained and free of imperfections. The remains of branches leave knots that warp the inner grain, so straight, limbless lower trunks are critical for the acoustical quality and structural integrity of tonewood.

Antoine Cauche also spoke of using maple from the Balkans, as did the golden age violin makers. There are three maple species used for stringed instruments in Europe: sycamore maple, plane trees, and field maple. The most common source of maple for the quartet instruments is *Acer pseudoplatanus,* known as sycamore maple in America and simply as "sycamore" in the United Kingdom. In North America, "sycamore" is the name given to *Platanus occidentalis*. Often referred to as a plane tree in the United Kingdom, this species has a striking appearance characterized by patchy, peeling bark that has been likened to khaki camouflage. In Europe, plane trees are often seen lining country roads or shading canals. They survive in cities because they are more resistant to pollution than some other tree species. The peeling bark is the tree's way of cleansing itself.

While plane trees can grow to over 150 feet tall, the sycamore maple tops out at about 100 feet and spreads in a broad and round shape. The branches sometimes extend as wide as the tree is tall. Its distinctive pointed, five-lobed leaves turn bright orange, yellow, and red in the autumn, and the tree provides a sugary sap that is sometimes distilled for sycamore maple liqueur. Though the sycamore maple's native habitat is Central Europe and Western Asia, the tree finds its way into parks and along urban streets in the United Kingdom, North America, and Australia, and thrives in the countryside of such favorable places. It also enriches the colorful autumn palette of the Carpathian Mountains.

The sycamore maple is not a high-altitude tree or one requiring the rare conditions necessary for musical-instrument-grade spruce. It is sourced from the Balkans because large specimens grow there and lumber companies have freer access to them than they do in other European countries. While instrument-grade Norway spruce comes only from very specific mountain environments, the three species of maple commonly used in lutherie can be found throughout much of Central Europe. Like the finest spruce tonewood, however, flamed maple is rare and has its own mysteries and lore.

How do these common trees come to yield tonewood so rare and precious? What traditions lie behind this marriage of spruce and maple? The story of tonewood begins with one of the most specialized areas of lumbering and forestry and with one of the world's most precious natural resources: the forests themselves.

Marcello Mazzucchi, a poet and retired ranger for the Paneveggio violin forest in the Val di Fiemme, has developed an acute ear for—as the Stradivari myth would have it—knocking on a tree and divining whether it has a violin, viola, or cello inside. Amati and Guarneri were supposed to have acquired their spruce sound tables or bellies from the Paneveggio area as well. Little is actually known about lives and methods of the master instrument makers, and information about the early period in the evolution of the violin and associated bowed instruments remains fairly sketchy too. The most significant developments might well have occurred around Milan, which lies just south of the Italian Alps and their tonewood-producing forests.

The image of trees containing violins is seductive. In an Alaskan Sitka spruce forest, on the other hand, we might imagine trees with Steinway & Sons or Baldwin pianos inside them. Steinway's publicity boasts of its "diaphragmatic soundboard" and the materials exploited to make it. A Steinway piano "combine[s] the resonance of Sitka spruce with the rigidity of hard rock maple to intensify the richness of the sound."

Sitka spruce (*Picea sitchensis*) can provide resonance comparable to that of Norway spruce and is considered one of the choicest tonewoods by some of the iconic acoustic guitar–making companies, including Martin & Co., Gibson, and Taylor. Guitar backs and sides can be made from a wide variety of decorative woods, giving the instrument visual character and beauty. Sitka spruce also provided wood for airplanes in both world wars, the planes, like musical instruments, requiring significant tensile strength and lightness of materials. Thus it might be said that Sitka spruce trees also have airplanes inside them.

The acoustical marriage of spruce and maple captures the imagination and heart of those who love the depth, harmonics, power, and warmth characteristic of their instrumental offspring. Both a Steinway grand piano and a violin may owe their excellence to the sound velocity and sustained resonance of spruce and maple. For the quartet instruments and the double bass, however, it is also necessary to consider the importance of the bow to the quality of tone.

Bow making is a specialized art known as *archèterie*, the refinement of which occurred in France. *Archèterie* requires different materials from those used by the luthier, including carefully selected horsehair and—over the last few centuries—Pernambuco, or brazilwood. (Like Brazilian rosewood, Pernambuco is now considered endangered.)

If Norway spruce and sycamore maple are two common species in Europe, what makes them so desirable acoustically and aesthetically? The answer lies in the architecture of the trees. Norway spruce can grow up to 180 feet tall. Adirondack spruce and Engelmann spruce, both of which provide top-quality tonewood for guitars, violins, harps, and pianos, can reach 130 feet, with some exceptional trees growing considerably taller. Sitka spruce can attain the remarkable height of 300 feet. As a pillar, a Sitka spruce would match the height of the Statue of Liberty from base to torch.

Tree growth differs from that of humans and other animals in several ways. For one thing, trees develop a structure from the outside in, ideally building enough inner skeletal tissue each year to lend strength that defies gravity, strong winds, and snowstorms. Animals grow to limited sizes by shedding old, worn, and possibly damaged cells and structures. With trees, however, dead cells make up the rigid skeleton that endows them with form and strength, allowing them to become as large as their species permits.

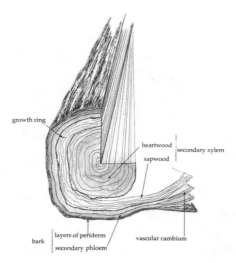

Cross section of a tree trunk. (Hélène Collandre)

The trunk of a tree displays radial symmetry, so to understand the growth of the trunk and how it uses dead cells, imagine a series of five belts—inner and outer ones—that encompass the trunk and run vertically up the trunk and branches. Every tree has, just under its bark, a belt of stem cells, called cambium, that will generate the two major types of wood. The cambium layers are very small in relation to the trunk—only a few inches thick. The cells that make up the inner layer facing the heart of the tree form a complex of vessels called xylem that serves to transport water up toward the leaves. While the xylem cells are living, they do the transporting job; as new xylem is formed, the older cells die but remain in place. These tubular xylem structures fill with resins and gums, which constitute the wood of the tree.

Two more belts occupy the space to the outside of the cambium. These cells are also tubular, and they also transport materials critical to the life of the tree. All the products of photosynthesis that have occurred in the leaves are transported down toward the roots by vascular tissue called phloem, with the same pattern of living and dead cells. Freshly generated phloem cells do the transporting work while their proximate outside neighbors die and are filled with resins, contributing to the bark of the tree.

How do these patterns of growth result in annual rings that permit us to know the number of years a tree has been around? Summer wood grows rapidly and has a pale color, while winter wood is formed more slowly and is denser and darker. Both types of rings are composed of dead xylem.

Enriched water is transported through the xylem into the branching crown, where it assists in photosynthesis and mostly evaporates. The xylem also transmits hormonal orders: "grow," "reproduce," "store," "stop growing," and "sleep." It is during the sleep phase that the best tonewood is cut.

For musical instruments, and with spruce in particular, the density of the rings also influences sound. Generally, the denser the ring pattern, the faster the sound velocity. Analysis of these growth rings gave rise to the science of dendrochronology, from which it is possible not only to determine the age of a tree by counting rings but also to identify anomalies that indicate the history of weather changes, fires, and other atmospheric influences.

For antique instrument appraisers, dendroarchaeology (a dendrochronology subspecialty) has become an invaluable tool for settling long-standing arguments about the authenticity of certain golden age Cremonese violins. Suspicions long persisted about the origin of the "Messiah," one of Stradivari's most celebrated violins. Doubts stem from its near perfect condition more than three centuries after its construction and from some variations in style. These anomalies led some to believe that the French luthier Jean-Baptiste Vuillaume, an important musical innovator, might have crafted it more than a hundred years after the period of Stradivari. Early dendrochronological analysis raised more questions than it answered, until a more sophisticated study was conducted by Henri D. Grissino-Mayer and colleagues using both comparisons to other instruments of the time and regional tree-ring chronology. The results not only confirmed the authenticity of the Stradivarius but also revealed that the belly of the instrument was derived from a spruce growing at a relatively low altitude, whereas the other Stradivarius instruments came from trees growing at an intermediate altitude.

Some experts speculate that the Little Ice Age that occurred during the Cremonese golden age of violin making contributed to a difference in the quality of the tonewood the masters used. Dendrochronology helps scientists establish the dates and the effects of this cold period and, in the middle of it, the Maunder Minimum, a period from 1645 to 1715 when there was greatly diminished sunspot activity, which also contributed to cooler temperatures.

This climate change manifested itself in advancing glaciers, frozen seaports, greatly shortened growing seasons, and receding tree lines. European paintings from the time, such as the frozen winter scenes of Pieter Bruegel, capture the effects of the Little Ice Age. Trees grown

at a lower altitude, such as the spruce used for the Messiah Stradivarius, experienced a shorter growing season, and the tree rings
are correspondingly tighter. In their paper "Stradivari, Violins, Tree
Rings, and the Maunder Minimum: A Hypothesis," Grissino-Mayer
and L. Berkle raise the possibility that cooler overall temperatures and
shorter summers during the Maunder Minimum caused slower, more
even tree growth. The climate change in concert with environmental
conditions, including disposition, elevation, and soil content, produced
stiff, light spruce with superior sound properties. Stradivari used wood
that came from the period of the Little Ice Age for instruments made
later in his life. Grissino-Mayer and Berkle point out that the climate
and environmental conditions of this period have not reoccurred
since Stradivari's greatest period of instrument making.

The Maunder Minimum is recorded in the grain of the "Macdonald"
Stradivarius viola, the "Duport" Stradivarius cello, and the "Vieuxtemps" Guarnerius violin, instruments whose combined value is as
much as $71 million. These instruments consist primarily of the cel-
lulose from dead xylem cells in spruce and maple filled with lignin, an
organic polymer that hardens, resists rot, and, with curing, grows ever
lighter until "every pore of the wood" is ready to be filled with music.

4

Cremona and the
Paneveggio Forest

TONEWOOD SOURCES FOR THE AMATI,
STRADIVARIUS, AND GUARNERIUS INSTRUMENTS

IN HIS ENCYCLOPEDIC BOOK *Bois de musique: La forêt berceau de l'harmonie,* published in 2004, Jean-Marie Ballu describes species of trees around the world that yield tonewood. He identifies specific woods used in different instruments and the cutting and milling techniques applied to carefully selected logs. In a section titled "The Atlas of Music Wood," Ballu provides maps showing areas where the principal tonewoods come from, dividing them into two categories: exotic wood, primarily from the tropics, and European wood. Two maps represent the European wood, one showing broad zones in Europe and Western Asia where field maple, sycamore, and Norway maple naturally occur. The second map pinpoints seven locations for spruce tonewood forests: Bolzano in Italy's Val de Fiemme, Risoux in both the French and Swiss Jura, Rougemont near Château d'Oeux in Switzerland, the forest areas near Salzburg, Austria, Reghin in northeastern Romania (Transylvania), Zakopane in southern Poland, and the Ore Mountains around Klatovy, Czech Republic.

The seven forest regions share four key characteristics that nurture instrument-quality spruce: altitude, temperatures, disposition to light, and soil composition. All of these locations fall within the Alps and the Carpathian Mountains, and all are places of particular importance to the evolution of instrument making. Some of them are sites with instrument-making schools or important workshops, along with a few major instrument factories. Several of these locations are close by vestiges of primeval forest, raising concerns about conservation and environmental protection. All of them support the lumber industry—with greater or lesser success—in maintaining sustainability. Tonewood milling is very specialized, in part because very old, large trees are required. Their selection and cutting provides a window onto the management and current health of the forests.

Since the forests are distributed through mountainous areas of different countries, both similarities and differences can be noted in the culture and traditions involved in stringed-instrument making. Jean-Louis Prochasson and Antoine Cauche would be the first to say that a new cooperative spirit is emerging in lutherie, one that extends internationally beyond fellow instrument makers to tonewood suppliers and musicians. Major international musical instrument expositions such as Musicora (Paris), Music China (Shanghai), and Musikmesse (Frankfurt) furnish a lively environment for contemporary luthiers, as do more intimate workshops and symposiums.

Among these musical expositions, Cremona Musica enjoys the advantage of being in a historic Italian city famed for lutherie. Besides the Cremona Musica International Exposition, the city concurrently hosts the Stradivari Festival and, every third year, the Antonio Stradivari International Triennale Violin Making Competition, described by *Strad* magazine as "the Olympics of violin-making." The exhibitions cover practically every aspect of stringed-instrument making.

The enormous exhibition center that accommodates the Cremona Musica is located along the northern loop of the city. Two pavilions house five programs: Cremona Mondomusica (stringed-instrument marketplace), the Piano Experience, the Acoustic Guitar Village, the Cremona Winds, and the Accordion Show. The exhibition includes thousands of instruments, both new and vintage—some made by iconic factories and others handmade, including an array of ethnic instruments, intriguing acoustical inventions, and works by contemporary master luthiers. The three-day schedule comprises more than 160 concerts, seminars, and master classes. Wide-eyed attendees stroll past stands of polished instruments, published music, and trade literature, in addition to such craft items as ingredients for varnishes and stains, ornate tuning keys, delicately shaped maple bridges of all sizes, strings, fine chisels, and carbon-fiber sound posts.

In many ways, the Piano Experience provides the most impressive part of the Cremona Musica program. It is purported to be the world's largest trade fair for pianos. A number of internationally celebrated pianists appear in sponsored festival performances, and many of the major piano companies are represented, including Bösendorfer, Fazioli, Petrof, Steingraeber, Steinway & Sons, and Yamaha. Models of the earliest Bartolomeo Cristofori and Anton Walter fortepianos are on display, enabling visitors to see and appreciate the heritage and evolution of keyboard instruments.

Pianos, despite their size and cost, are the world's most popular instrument, a popularity reflected in a surge in Chinese and South Korean manufacturing and domestic and export sales. By the 1920s there were well over a hundred piano makers in the United States alone. Some piano companies have had a significant impact on the industrial histories of the countries in which they were produced.

Yamaha started as a piano and reed-organ manufacturing company in 1887, and today maintains an impressive reputation for producing high-quality instruments. In a post–World War II transition, the company transformed from a piano manufacturer into an international conglomerate producing motorcycles and lawn mowers, along with instruments for the entire orchestra, pianos, guitars, and synthesizers. Like its fellow Japanese piano company Kawai, Yamaha today acquires soundboard Sitka spruce from Alaska.

Some of the world's most notable piano makers were established in the early to mid-nineteenth century. These include Bösendorfer, Pleyel, Blüthner, Bechstein, and Steinway & Sons, each making its own particular contributions to nuances of voice and playability. Steinway & Sons presents an intriguing case since it manufactured pianos in both New York and Hamburg, and instruments from the two factories possess distinct differences dictated by musical tradition and the materials used in their construction.

The story of the German American instrument maker Heinrich Egelhard Steinweg, later Henry E. Steinway, borders on mythic. Steinweg survived being struck by a lightning bolt that killed his brother and father and left him temporarily deaf. He became a carpenter and an organ-maker's apprentice. Regaining his hearing, he became an organist and then a luthier before making his first grand piano—in his kitchen. In 1850 Steinweg emigrated to the United States, changed his name to Steinway, worked briefly for a piano manufacturer, and then started his own company with his sons. Steinway & Sons pianos won first prize in major competitions in New York, London, and Paris, elevating the company's international reputation and expansion, leading to a factory in Hamburg designed to meet European demand.

At the Steinway factory in Astoria, Queens, visitors learn not only that each handmade piano is imbued with its own distinct sound (like a great violin), but also that there are larger categorical differences between the sound of a Hamburg Steinway and one made in New York. European classical taste is thought to favor a lush and clear voice, versus the more commanding one Americans prefer, which will permit a pianist playing Gershwin to cut through an orchestra in a large auditorium. While in recent years, Steinway & Sons has aimed to close the gap on the tonal contrasts between the pianos made in the United States and Germany, piano sellers and restorers still note such differences as the felt used on the hammers (harder and softer felt and adjustments for voicing), the hammer mechanisms themselves (which come only from Renner in Germany), and the makers of strings. The

difference in materials comes first through the choice of expert build-
ers: Steinways made in New York feature Sitka spruce soundboards
and hard maple framing; Hamburg instruments are made of alpine
Norway spruce, beech, and different maple species.

Piano factories mill their own wood. In "Seeking the Perfect Piano
Piece, in Spruce," James Barron notes that "Steinway's lumberyard is
a temporary home to millions of dollars' worth of wood—birch, maple,
spruce, poplar. Some of it is earmarked for sounding boards, some for
lids, some for wrest planks, the thick chunks of laminated wood that
are also known as pin blocks (a pin block holds the pins that tuners
twist to bring a note up to its pitch, or take it down)." The wood that the
Hamburg factory of Steinway & Sons uses comes from the European
forests that Ballu names in Bavaria and the Alps in his tonewood maps
of Europe. At Cremona Musica, tonewood milling companies located
near these forests sell billets, some specializing in guitars and others
in the whole spectrum of stringed instruments: Tonholz (Germany),
Bachmann (Italy), Drewbas (Poland), Tonewood (Switzerland), and
Topwood (Romania), to name a few. Buyers, many of whom are Asian,
run their fingers across the book matched pieces, judge their weight,
and hold them near their ears as they tap on them. They inspect the
tightness of the grain and look over the figuring. Some carry electronic
gauges with them to measure sound velocity.

Cacophony surges as the programs reach full force. Vendors demonstrate instruments, buyers test them at the stands or in the designated
"Red Room" space, and concerts get under way, some in the Salle Cristofori. The exhibition awards are given mostly for performance and
communication. However, one is designated for guitar lutherie, the 2018
prize going to Hermann Hauser III from Bavaria. The Hauser family
is beginning its fifth generation of luthiers with Hermann Hauser III's
daughter, Kathrin Hauser, now learning her forefathers' art.

The quality guitar making of Hermann Hauser Sr., second in line,
caught the attention of Andrés Segovia. While traveling in Germany,
Segovia met Hauser Sr. and showed him his Spanish Ramirez guitar.

Hauser took measurements for three hours. However, when Segovia tried the guitar Hauser made for him, he was unimpressed by the sound, though he said the instrument was very beautiful. While violin makers are fond of using adjectives such as "heart-piercing," "eloquent," "wafting," "sensuous," and "solemn" to describe an instrument's sound, Segovia often used nouns: "color," "timbre," "harmonics," "polyphony," "soul." Segovia felt the Hauser guitar that he was presented with was "a very faithful copy, but with no soul." He loved the treble but felt that the bass was shallow. Hauser understood Segovia's concerns, and this exchange initiated a twelve-year collaboration between musician and luthier to achieve an ideal instrument. Hauser would send one or two guitars to Segovia each year, but none was quite right. Ultimately, it was worth the wait when in 1937 Hauser produced a guitar with German spruce top and Brazilian rosewood back and sides. Segovia called the instrument "the greatest guitar of our epoch." He performed and recorded with it between 1937 and 1962. Unfortunately, the guitar was damaged in a recording studio accident involving a microphone, and Segovia mourned the change in sound quality. Nevertheless, the guitar is now in the possession of the Metropolitan Museum of Art.

One wonders what Amati, Guarneri, and Stradivari would think if given VIP passes to Cremona Musica. Their master classes would be overflowing and broadcast worldwide, not least because the exquisite acoustics of their instruments remain a mystery. Why did these violins improve with age, likely far beyond their creators' expectations?

Amati, Stradivari, and Guarneri all chiseled, glued, and varnished their masterpieces in a setting devoted to artistic and architectural accomplishment, thanks to the combined wealth and power of the aristocracy and the Catholic Church. It is fitting that the Cremona Violin Museum shares the heart of the city with the twelfth-century cattedrale di Santa Maria Assunta e San Gottardo and its medieval octagonal baptistry along with the Torrazzo, a decorated brick bell tower with the world's largest astronomical clock. The previous Stradivarius

Museum was more modest, consisting of only three rooms, one of which included the templates for tops, forms for bending and gluing side wood, instrument plans, and tools. These historical tools have been incorporated into the current Museo del Violino, which is housed in the Palazzo dell'Arte, a building originally constructed during the Fascist era. With funding from the Italian steel magnate Giovanni Arvedi and an interior design by Giorgio Palù, the structure was renovated to house the new high-tech and interactive museum.

A visit there begins with a short tunnel displaying examples of the earliest versions of the violin and cello, along with video projections covering the origins of the violin. Visitors are cautioned that its invention should not be attributed to any one Renaissance luthier. The introduction is followed by a recreation of Stradivari's workshop. Displays show that he penned his notes on his top templates and used circular measurements for the placement of f-holes and lines for the bass bar. His notes also appear on his thick walnut wood forms, and experts are still working to decipher them, hampered by the paucity of Stradivari's writings extant today. The exhibition reveals a great craftsman continually experimenting, making infinitesimal changes, never quite content. It also shows that methods have hardly changed in three hundred years. Luthiers and fine tonewood experts say you need to start with a design: at this museum you could lean over the glass cases and gaze at the most famous ones.

Anyone seeking to understand the history of the violin's evolution should, if at all possible, try to see the lavish baroque fresco *Concerto degli Angeli* by Gaudenzio Ferrari, in the cupola of the Santuario di Saronno, a hundred miles northwest of Cremona. In 1530, Ferrari painted an impressive fifty-six instruments being played by a swirl of welcoming angels in Paradise. Emanuel Winternitz in "The School of Gaudenzio Ferrari and the Early History of the Violin" identifies the stringed instruments among them as "viols, several liras da braccio, rebecs, a Sicilian cane violin, a bizarre compound of fiddle with recorder, to be blown and bowed at the same time, and last but not least, a number of instruments that show most if not all of the basic characteristics of a violin." Winternitz emphasizes that the violin was not an invention per se but rather an amalgamation of design patterns and potentials of bowed instruments. In her book *The Cello,* the art historian Elizabeth Cowling analyzes early cello-like images in Ferrari's painting, compares them in size to the ones made by Andrea Amati, and suggests that on the basis of these early specimens we should hesitate to recognize Amati as the inventor of the cello.

Because stringed instruments are made out of wood and are therefore ephemeral, few early examples exist for archaeologists and musicologists to study their development and origins. The lyre is an exception since it appears in so much ancient iconography and early versions exist. The earliest extant examples of the lyre date to ancient Sumer. Among the most famous are the Lyres of Ur (2550–2450 BCE), buried in the Royal Cemetery among the many rows of women interred there. One specimen, known as "the Queen's Lyre," was found in a woman's hand bones, placed as if she were still playing it. Forms of the lyre and the related cithara can be found throughout the world, including bowed versions that developed across Europe, such as the Shetland *gue* and the Welsh *crwth,* both among the oldest traditional instruments. The *crwth* can be played somewhat like a viola da gamba, the cello's baroque precursor. Several instruments have been identified as key ancestors of the violin, including the rebec, which came to Europe through the Arab world; and the lira da braccio, a descendant of the medieval vielle.

Developments in violin making occurred rapidly in Northern Italy during the Renaissance, with luthiers working not only in the Brescia and Cremona areas but also in Milan and Venice. In fact, the concentration of venues, composers, and instrument makers in these areas throughout the eighteenth century and into the early nineteenth is astonishing. Aristocratic demand and patronage, most notably from the

Medici family, played no small role. Lorenzo de Medici commissioned the first violin in 1555 from Andrea Amati. In a letter to the master, Lorenzo stated that the instrument was to be "made of the highest quality materials like that of a lute, but simple to play." Amati is also credited with crafting in 1538 the first cello, named "The King." He fashioned a set of violins believed to have been gifts for the marriage of Philip II of Spain and Elisabeth of Valois. In 1560, Catherine de Medici, the regent queen of France, ordered thirty-eight instruments, obliging Amati to make violins, violas, and cellos in a range of sizes.

In Northern Italy, the popular composer Claudio Monteverdi wrote his revolutionary *La favola d'Orfeo* for the Mantua courts. It is now widely considered the work that transformed opera from large-scale baroque religious choirs to the Renaissance structure of story and songs. Venice was home to the much-loved Antonio Vivaldi, who composed forty-five operas. By the early eighteenth century, Venice had seven opera houses, the Teatro San Benedetto being the most prominent among them. After a fire destroyed the structure, the larger and more elegant Teatro La Fenice (The Phoenix) became Venice's premier opera showcase. Even the orphanages provided venues for great music. Milan's Teatro Regio Ducal opened in 1717; after it burned during a carnival night in 1776, wealthy Milanese patrons commissioned the building of the world-renowned La Scala.

In his chapter "The Renaissance (1400–1600)" in *The History of Musical Instruments,* the German musicologist Curt Sachs asserts that "the most outstanding development in the history of music between 1400–1600 is the emancipation of instrumental from vocal music. . . . Gradually, instruments took possession of all kinds of vocal forms." The quartet stringed instruments changed quickly and dramatically, as did the works of those composing for them. The predecessors of the piano were rapidly evolving at this time, too, starting with the clavichord in the fourteenth century, followed by the harpsichord, so important in the baroque period. The closest relative of the modern piano, the fortepiano, was invented in the middle of the golden era of violin making. Instruments were developing that would sing, converse, and meditate in a wide variety of voices.

Did Amati answer the call for a more dynamic version of a bowed instrument, or did the evolution of the violin naturally lead to the possibility of a more vibrant, forceful, and elaborate sound? Perhaps the answer lay in both demand and the development of form. After Amati and his sons had established the form of the violin as we know it, Stradivari experimented further, including a progression from the earlier long and narrow instruments to the shorter and wider-bodied ones typical of his golden period in the 1700s.

At the heart of the Violin Museum is the "Treasure Box," where visitors are greeted by the great Stradivarius Stauffer ex Cristiani 1700 cello, standing upright and suspended by thin filaments. The instrument exhibits some wear in the varnish on the vaulted flamed-maple back and the shoulder where it was clasped to the musician's body. The spruce top has fine black purfling very close to the bout edges and beautiful straight grain, the finest lines in the center. Every millimeter of grain, every nick and microcrack, every embedded particle has been analyzed, measured, and mapped in daylight and under ultraviolet light, with calipers and magnetic thickness gauges. X-ray fluorescent spectroscopy has identified sulfur, chlorine, potassium, bismuth, and zirconium in the varnish, along with some iron in the purfling. The intense scrutiny to which Stradivarius instruments were and are subjected has given rise to endless theories explaining their unmatched sound quality: varnish brews, preservative minerals used to prevent mold during stockage, wood cured in river water, and so on.

The Stauffer ex Cristiani 1700 cello leads the spotlit Amati, Stradivari, and Guarneri instruments, lined up in rows of two, delicately suspended behind the cello. Some have one-piece backs, some are yellow-stained, some have quilted figuring rather than flame. The Treasure Box is followed by exhibits of early luthier's tools and molds and finally the glass-encased displays of recent high-end violins, violas, cellos, and basses created by contemporary prize-winning luthiers. The museum provides a recording of each instrument being played so that visitors can appreciate its individual voice. Antoine Cauche's gold-medal winner for the Simone Sacconi Prize is displayed among the violas. These exceptional modern instruments were selected for inclusion on the basis of the same characteristics enumerated by historical musicologist Wendy Powers when she listed the criteria for evaluating the Metropolitan Museum of Art's collection of Cremonese instruments: "Tone, responsiveness, elegance of design, visual appeal, and precision of their craft."

Antonio Stradivari died at age ninety-five in 1737, and his sons and Guarneri del Gesù died shortly thereafter. The Cremonese golden age of lutherie at last came to an end with the death of the great violin maker Carlos Bergonzi. Advances in the design of the instrument and its bow now began to arise from the French school of Nicholas Lupot and Jean-Baptiste Vuillaume. In Lorraine, the commune of Mirecourt became one of the most influential centers for lutherie, producing numerous notable instruments as early as 1635. Many of the greatest specimens of the period, however, were left in convents, dusty aristocratic storage, or attics, their owners possessing little understanding of their value. Luigi Tarisio, a modest furniture maker and amateur violinist who lived in the early part of the nineteenth century, possessed an intimate understanding of the acoustical properties and value of forsaken violins, and became legendary for his recovery of some of the greatest Cremonese instruments. The fact that some of today's most gifted musicians are able to play some of the golden era masterpieces is a tribute to the intrepid Tarisio, who transported sacks of violins on foot from Northern Italy to Paris for evaluation and restoration. The "Messiah" Stradivarius was among his most prized possessions right up until his death, and his worshipful attitude toward the instrument is in part responsible for its near-pristine condition today.

One hundred fifty miles northeast of Cremona lies the Val di Fiemme and its storied Paneveggio forest, more informally known as the

Stradivarius Forest or "*la foresta dei violini*." The Paneveggio enjoys a microclimate conducive to the production of spruce with ideal acoustical properties. Aaron S. Allen, director of the Environment and Sustainability Program at the University of North Carolina, Greensboro, writes that from the Paneveggio "in the eighteenth century, the wood of the spruce embarked on a long and arduous, yet delicate and fortune-dependent, journey: musical trees of the mountain-valley forests were brought to nearby cities, where luthiers transformed them into musical instruments for use in concert halls, where the imaginations of countless audiences have been transfixed for centuries."

A trip from Cremona to the Paneveggio involves a journey through areas rich in musical tradition and provides an awareness of both the difficulties of and resources for transporting logs. To get to the forest, a traveler heads thirty-five miles north to Brescia, where master luthiers Gasparo Bertolotti and Giovanni Paolo Maggini worked on their key contributions to the violin's evolution. Dendroarchaeological studies conducted by Peter Ratcliff revealed that Brescia continued for some time as an active violin-making center after the deaths of Bertolotti and Maggini. In a *Nature Magazine* interview, Ratcliff commented that "large violins of the Brescian school, which have a double line of inlaid decoration, were thought to have faded out with the death of maker Giovanni Paolo Maggini in about 1630. But I have tested 4 of these instruments and found that they were made at least 50 years after his death." From Brescia, the route turns east, passing near Lake Garda, where Gasparo Bertolotti was born, and then on to Verona, not only the setting of Shakespeare's *Romeo and Juliet* and *Two Gentleman of Verona* but also home to many composers and the site of the Arena di Verona Opera Festival, held in a Roman amphitheater.

The Adige river passes through Verona. It is Italy's second longest river after the Po; both rivers reach the Venetian Lagoon delta area immediately south of Venice. The connection of Adige that runs through large forested areas in the Dolomite mountain range and the

Po provided an important log-driving route in the past. Modest mountain communes historically were dependent on the sale of timber for ship building, fuel, furniture, and housing. Wood for great musical instruments came via the same route, Cremona being situated on the Po. The Avisio river, a tributary of the Adige, follows the Val di Fiemme to the Paneveggio forest.

Along the Avisio, the communes have erected semi-abstract sculptures at each intersection roundabout showing the outline of one edge of a violin. The area depends economically on skiing and hiking, but also on the Sounds of the Dolomites Festival, which, inspired by the famed tonewood of the Paneveggio forest, lures tourists at the end of the summer. Concerts boasting internationally renowned musicians are held in the mountains, some at high-altitude refuges and passes, the goal being to create an experience in which music is bonded to nature. Families can spread out picnic blankets in front of musicians playing at seven thousand feet against a backdrop of prismatic Dolomite peaks. Each year a famous violinist is invited to walk among the Paneveggio forest trees and choose one from which his own instrument will be made—an interesting proposition since it might take a decade, or two or three, for a tree to be processed and aged into the best tonewood.

The present natural park is relatively small, covering 197 square miles. The altitude in different parts of the park varies by three thousand feet, and while Norway spruce accounts for 85 percent of the forest, beech, silver fir, Swiss pines, and sycamore maples can be found at lower altitudes, and larch tends to dominate the highest points. The forest has been respected for centuries as a logging resource and has been skillfully managed for productivity and sustainability.

After the time of Charlemagne, much of the region was controlled by counts supported by the Holy Roman Empire. In the fourteenth century the land fell into the possession of the House of Habsburg, where it remained for five centuries. While wood was exploited for construction and other uses in Venice and the surrounding area—and parts of the

Val di Fiemme forests were also leased to foreign interests—the local inhabitants benefited too: they were allowed timber for the construction and renovation of churches, and for their own needs.

So dependent were the fourteenth-century Venetians on wood and resources from their northern mountain-dwelling neighbors that they dubbed the Val di Fiemme their "magnificent sister," which evolved into the traditional name La Magnifica Comunità di Fiemme. As a Mediterranean trading power for centuries, Venice depended on timber for both naval and merchant ship building, yet the timber needs were far more extensive for the pylon construction that supports the city on its lagoon.

In the nineteenth century, inhabitants of Val di Fiemme began to enjoy more autonomy, and to profit as a commune from wood exploitation. We see this economic change, a kind of taxation, occur in mountain forest communities in France and Switzerland. Although the Paneveggio forest was well managed, it suffered during World War I. In combat zones, lines were formed with trenches and compounds in the forest, which then suffered from artillery fire, shrapnel, and bullets. After the war, the Italian government took possession of the forest, and swaths of woodland were felled in a salvaging operation equal to decades' worth of selective cutting. In addition to war damage, the Val di Fiemme trees suffered from waves of storms and the now-entrenched bark beetle epidemic.

The Autonomous Province of Trento established Paneveggio National Regional Park in 1967, giving it state-protected status. Contemporary forestry authorities impose varying levels of restriction throughout the park to protect tree repopulation projects and to promote sustainability. (Picking mushrooms, for example, is prohibited.) One of the busy assistants in the restoration process is the spotted nutcracker, which likes to store excess pine nuts but sometimes forgets them, inadvertently becoming a violin forest propagator.

Spruce trees in the Paneveggio display several interesting characteristics. For one thing, they tend to form tight communities, shading out other species. The community's growth is so compact that the trees lose their lower branches as they grow in soaring columns up to their crowns. Perhaps the most astonishing feature is how a 140-foot violin tree could support itself in alpine rockfall. Such a tree's roots look like the arms of an octopus as they grip a shallow layer of earth around rocks or snake into fissures. The rocky soil also supports abundant moss, which possesses a startling capacity for holding water, somewhere between twenty and a hundred times its own weight. Norway spruce loves water, and moss plays an important role in keeping the soil moist.

On October 29, 2018, Storm Adrian, the most powerful storm to strike Italy in decades, hit the region. It lasted three days, bringing with it winds of well over one hundred miles per hour. The storm flooded 75 percent of Venice and killed thirty people. Much of the Paneveggio forest was leveled. The *Strad* news reported:

> Storms in the Italian Dolomites last week have flattened large portions of Alpine forest—the source of the spruce wood favored by Antonio Stradivari for making violins.
>
> Winds of up to 110 mph uprooted over 1.5 million trees in the Trentino area, leaving many of them dangling from power lines. One of the worst hit areas was Paneveggio park, where Stradivari selected wood for his instruments.

Bruno Crosignani, director of the office of the Panaveggio Forest that manages the harvesting of tonewood, termed the damage to the forest "unprecedented." Videos and photographs show whole mountain slopes looking as if a gigantic scythe had swept through. The trees all fell in one direction.

Many factors came together to result in such extensive damage to the forest. One theory suggests that restoration was partly responsible. Joy Lo Dico, writing in *Financial Times*, commented that "the Dolomites were the scene of bitter fighting in glacial conditions and the banks down this valley were cleared of their trees for sightlines. The front ran through it in 1917. When peace came, the crops of spruce grew back together naturally. All were around the same height and age. 100 years on, together they were felled by the wind."

Nevertheless, while large tracts of the forest will not be harvestable for decades, its salvaged wood will continue to find its way into churches, chalets, and musical instruments. The tonewood company Ciresa, based near Cavalese, has been trying to salvage as much of the instrument-quality wood as possible.

5

The Franco-Swiss Jura Mountains

THE FOREST AS A RENEWABLE GARDEN

THE JURA MOUNTAIN CHAIN runs roughly south-north along the France-Switzerland border, between the Rhone and the Rhine rivers. In the southern range of the mountains, a dominant cliff face, the Salève, offers a view of geological stratification created during the Middle/Upper Jurassic and the Lower Cretaceous periods. The term "Jurassic" is in fact derived from the Jura mountain range, where the German geologist and paleontologist Leopold von Buch was able to identify stone strata created between 201.3 and 145 million years ago. "Jura" comes from the Latinized Celtic word *Juria*, meaning forest, and it now identifies not only a mountain range but also a department in eastern France.

While von Buch is today remembered primarily for his work on the Jurassic period, he had a significant role in the early nineteenth-century neptunist and plutonist controversy, determining whether rock was created by sediment crystallization occurring in the ocean or by volcanic activity. Von Buch was one of the early geologists to survey the Dolomites, producing a highly detailed map that shows the distribution of limestone (calcium carbonate) and dolostone (calcium magnesium carbonate). While studying the differences between the two rocks formed by carbonate precipitation, he began to doubt his own neptunist convictions when considering that volcanic activity may have introduced magnesium into limestone. He would later argue for a volcanic explanation based on dolostone findings in Ireland. But what caused the assimilation of magnesium and the formation of the more stable dolostone, the one more resistant to acids that can form in rain, remains to be explained. Some propose that dolostone comes from sediments in environments of higher salinity, such as lagoons, while others contend that microbes contributed to the mineral formation. Like the limestone that characterizes the area around the Paneveggio forest, the Jura was formed in part by a raised epicontinental shallow sea.

While the Alps present the spectacular grandeur of rugged peaks and glaciers, the French Parc naturel régional du Haut-Jura and the contiguous Swiss Parc naturel régional Jura vaudois reveal subtler beauties: mountain lakes, lines of limestone cliff faces showing through forests, and small ravines with waterfalls. The French park also includes a wildlife preserve. Geologists refer to formation of the Jura as "folded," meaning the land mass thrusts upward and literally curls itself along faults. These subterranean pressures, along with streams carving and tunneling through limestone, create the karstic phenomena resulting in steep head valleys, chasms, cave vaults, plateaus, and escarpments. You can see folds in the striations, a rippling archlike effect called an anticline that resembles ribbon candy. The Jura chain straddles the France-Switzerland border up to Zurich and serves partially as a watershed for two great European rivers: the Rhine, flowing across Westphalia and Holland to the North Sea, and the Rhone, running in the opposite direction through southeastern France to the Mediterranean.

Products such as Comté and Vacherin cheeses, Arbois wine (often called straw wine from its color), spiced and herbal Morteau sausage, dried cèpe and morel mushrooms, and "green fairy" absinthe contribute to regional identity. Woodworking industries and crafts still thrive, turning out split shingles, furniture, cabinets, cooking tools, tobacco pipes, slivered wood to box runny cheese, and tonewood for acoustical instruments. Managed logging is evident throughout the mountains. Logs are stacked on flatbed rail cars, loaded on trucks, or piled in lumberyards, to be cured under jets of water. Much of the wood is Norway spruce, and foresters with an eye for music trees have historically worked in several small forests in the Jura. Notable among these are the forests of Risoux—which is also a part of the Swiss parklands—and Massacre, which lies on the far side of the French town of Les Rousses.

Historical episodes left their mark in this area. The Massacre forest acquired its name from a sixteenth-century military disaster that befell six hundred Italian mercenaries whom Francis I of France had sent to break a Savoyard siege of Geneva. The Savoyards stopped them at the Faucille Pass. After a disorganized retreat, the mercenaries dispersed and were brutally murdered in the forest for which they are remembered. The Risoux forest served to shelter resistance operatives and conceal Jews escaping France during World War II. In 2015 a monument was erected to honor the small cadre of men and women, Swiss and French, who worked together to save lives.

These forests, a mere ten miles from each other, are both part of the Parc naturel régional du Haut-Jura. Like the Dolomites, they enjoy ideal environmental and climatic conditions for the production of high-quality Norway spruce. The forest nurtures trees that can be as much as two hundred years old and rise to a height of 160 feet.

In the Franche Comté village of Fertans (population under three hundred), forester Bernard Michaud created le Bois de lutherie, one of the most respected tonewood milling and distributing enterprises in Europe. The company's distribution is international and includes North America and Asia. Michaud started out as a woodcutter without a musical background, but after years of working in the Haut-Jura, he developed an awareness of and appreciation for the exceptional qualities of the local Norway spruce and began to concentrate on tonewood production. Le Bois de lutherie evolved as Michaud began consulting expert luthiers, most notably Philippe Bodart from nearby Besançon and Jean-Christophe Graff from Strasbourg. The tonewood lumber mill now includes an impressive craft center that offers instrument-making workshops and hosts conferences. Versions of those workshops are now offered in Romania, and Michaud travels throughout Europe to instrument festivals to supply and consult luthiers.

Michaud initially invited me to meet him in the Risoux forest but had to change plans because of a meeting at his workshop, so he asked me to join him in Fertans instead. Le Bois de lutherie consists mainly of two buildings situated on the rue de la Scierie (Sawmill Road). The first is a large shed that houses sawmill machinery, stacked logs in various stages of processing, and space for aging wood. The other building houses luthier workshop benches and tools, an office, and two floors for stocking processed wood. Bernard Michaud defies anyone's clichéd image of the burly, flannel-clad woodcutter. He is wiry and very clever. In fact, he fits the image that luthier Patrick Robin conjured for music wood: "The best spruce is like the mountain people, light and very strong."

Michaud had finished lunch with the three master luthiers, who filtered back to the workshop to carve their instruments, and then he took me on a tour of his sawmill shed and the workshops. "We follow two different strategies when it comes to figured maple and Norway spruce," he remarked. "Maple with attractive waves and structure can be found almost anywhere. One can cut it in France, Bosnia, or Romania. You have to look for very large trees with rare patterns in their grain, and we locate them through our network of forestry contacts. When it comes to Norway spruce, however, we chose trees in especially beautiful areas, always in the same places. We find many potential tonewood trees in the Risoux forest and the Massacre forest, which is a little south. What is particular about these forests is their altitude—more than three thousand feet—and the long tradition of silviculture practiced in each. It is like *jardinage* [gardening]."

Michaud used the analogy of gardening repeatedly to convey the practical and environmental foundation of silviculture, which is to maintain the growth, health, and quality of the forest. France takes well-deserved pride in its forests and has practiced careful management for centuries. For example, the Landes forest, the largest in France, consists predominantly of maritime pines that were planted expressly as part of a vast project to transform swamps and marshlands and protect Bordeaux's vineyards by tempering cold fronts coming off the ocean. The Landes forest is also an important source of pine resin, which is distilled for bow-hair rosin and fine violin varnish. The cultivation and management of forest resources does indeed take on the more intimate sense of gardening, but above all, Michaud wanted to emphasize forestry tradition.

"A stability is being maintained in these forests. A balance of young, middle, and old trees must be kept, and the best trees selected for cutting will be replaced in ten to twenty years by others." Lumbering operations can quickly profit from cutting trees of all ages, but this, Michaud maintains, does not provide quality wood. The practice has led to disastrous strip clearcutting in some of Europe's most important forests. In the United States, the lumber industry has destroyed entire white pine forests in the Northeast, and the redwood and Sitka spruce resources are being seriously damaged. When I referred to the deforestation that has plagued areas of the Czech Republic, Michaud added that forests in Poland and Romania have also suffered from severe clearcutting. "*Coup définitif,*" he called it. "It's a serious problem as quality wood is becoming rarer."

When I suggested that new tonewood sources might be found in Russia or Ukraine, Michaud replied with conviction that tradition makes a critical difference. "It's the same with wine. You can produce red wine anywhere, but in Burgundy, for example, the *terroir* is very favorable. And there is expertise." The term *terroir* carries important implications in French—in a sense, it covers everything that characterizes a place.

French forestry tradition has long depended on the *garde forestiers,* government-certified forest rangers whose responsibilities include carefully monitoring and maintaining forests that they come to know intimately. The garde forestiers police these forests and their integrated farms to protect from pollution, poaching, and the abusive exploitation of plants and trees. They work in concert with woodcutters, providing information that will help the latter maintain the stable health and future stability of the forest. This involves selecting and rotating work in sectors. In a sense, the garde forestier is the head gardener of the forest.

It would be reasonable to expect similarities between the Jura and the long-recognized tonewood forests around the Swiss villages of Rougemont and Château-d'Oex. As the crow flies, they're about eighty miles apart. Michaud refuted this, however. "They are quite different. The Risoux forest is almost flat, a plateau, where the climate and the geography are especially favorable for tonewood trees. The vegetation period, the phase during which the tree produces cellulose, is very short, and the winters are cold and wet." The stop-and-go growth creates tight tree rings, the signature feature of the resonant top wood on fine quartet instruments. Michaud continued, "In contrast, the Alps are sharply sloped, and the weather is more unpredictable. The trees grow under harsher, less favorable conditions."

Norway spruce are somewhat finicky, preferring an acidic soil pH level of about 5.5. However, though it takes a little time, trees possess the ability to adjust soil acidity to their preferred levels through calcium deposited from fallen leaves. Norway spruce live in harmony with larch and Swiss stone pine at high altitudes, and with a broad variety of trees at lower ones. They seem to thrive in the company of mycorrhizal fungi—that is, fungi with the ability to interact symbiotically with a tree's root system. Spruce appear to barter energy-giving sugars produced by photosynthesis for fungal water and minerals.

As Michaud and I passed through the mill shed, he pointed out numerous cuts of wood, commenting, "We always buy wood in October and bring it here." I had understood that the colder months with less movement of sap would be better, but Michaud informed me that the Risoux and Massacre forests had protections. "You can't cut in the snow," he said reprovingly. "It is forbidden to disturb the snow in a nature reserve." This represents a significant change from earlier times, when loggers took advantage of snow and ice to help oxen or workhorses drag massive logs to rivers or by using sturdy carts. The ground and networks of mycelium were thus disturbed. Now experts understand the importance of maintaining organic soil structure for the health of the forest.

Michaud stood holding two billets next to a log, and demonstrated where they came from. "We cut the wood just like a tart." By this he meant quarter cut—wedges with the vortex at the center of the log. "We make twins this way, billets for symmetry, like these for a viola top." He held the two wedges of wood cut together to show how the grain matched, opening them like a book. This cut is standard in both spruce and maple for the belly and the maple back respectively of a stringed instrument so that the grain matches. It should be noted that while matching billets are fairly standard in the violin family instruments, many tops and backs on Stradivarius instruments were carved from single pieces of wood. Experts have also discovered that up to sixteen of Stradivari's instruments used wood from the same tree.

Michaud showed me that each billet carries a stamp, something like a brand, along with cataloguing numbers for age and quality. "The wood is certified for age. Luthiers want wood that has been aged for at least four, five, six, ten years." Michaud pointed to different wood types he sells—among them cypress, linden, and poplar—and names the instruments of which they are destined to become a part. "This is maple for a double bass, and here is walnut used for making an electric guitar. This spruce will be used for a harpsichord. And this is dogwood for a flute. Dogwood is very hard and can be used in place of ebony." Now that ebony is among the protected endangered tree species, instrument makers are forced to find alternatives.

Leaving the shed, Michaud picked up a scrap of maple and snapped it along the grain. When he shifted the wood in the sunlight, the wavy iridescence glowed silver, like the sea in bright angled sunlight. When curly maple has been crafted into furniture or an instrument, it produces a mesmerizing three-dimensional illusion. "Only one tree in a thousand has this fiber," Michaud announced proudly. "It is very rare."

As we walked through the stock rooms, he pointed out several pairs of billets destined to become guitar tops. He explained, "The fine-grained tops are more suited to classical, folk, or other guitars used extensively for fingerpicking. For a western-style acoustic guitar, you probably would want a rounder, deeper grain for a warmer sound." These comments seemed to reflect luthier Prochasson's preference for wider-grain tops for cellos when I spoke to him about his version of the Stauffer ex Cristiani 1700 cello. Among guitar luthiers, there is considerable debate about the acoustical qualities based on density of the grain, with other key factors such as flexibility and weight credited.

Michaud carefully inspected stacked pairs of top wood, the matching pieces featuring a carefully drawn outline of a guitar body. As objects alone, the plates were decorative enough to hang on a wall. Michaud pinpointed the source. "This wood comes from Risol, a little north between Mouthe and Chapelle des Bois. This is a very small parcel within Risoux." He possesses an intimate knowledge of the nearby forests and uncanny intuitive powers for choosing trees with the potential for resonant wood. He studies their shape and the circumstances of their growth, and sees imaginatively into their trunks.

Michaud's imagination extends even further. As he once remarked in an interview, "I pick up everything weird," explaining that there are always specialists or people with a hobby who need materials for a cricket bat, a sculpture, an antique instrument, or any number of other purposes. In fact, le Bois de lutherie once held an archery bow–making workshop. (Coincidentally, some musicologists think that the archery bow was also among the oldest musical instruments.) All in all, Michaud sees potential beyond the forest in creating an international center that connects nature, top-class musicians, students, and the best handcraft experts.

He maintains his meticulously organized merchandise in stock rooms adjacent to the lutherie workshop area. One day, a small group of master luthiers were participating in what Michaud called "a meeting." Antoine Lescombe was busy at one bench carving a violin top. At the time, he was serving as the president of l'Association des luthiers et archetiers pour le développement de la facture instrumentale du quatuor. At another bench, Andrea Frandsen from Angers was also crafting a violin.

Michaud only half-jokingly said, "Angers is now the capital of lutherie. For 'the last cause,' we are obligated to go to Angers. And the weather is better there." (His allusion to "the last cause" may have come from Descartes' analogy that all philosophy is like a tree that culminates in wisdom: its fruit is the luthiers of Angers.) Michaud went on to say that the present "meeting" was an opportunity for master luthiers to share techniques, experiences, and ideas with each other. One might expect luthiers to guard trade secrets carefully, but, said Michaud, "That was the old generation. The new one is much more open to an exchange of ideas." Michaud was friends with Patrick Robin and Andrea Frandsen, both of whom mentored Antoine Cauche for seven years.

Frandsen, one of those present, lives and works a mere two kilometers across the Loire from Cauche's workshop in Angers. She explained to me how she became a luthier after growing up in rural Denmark, where there was very little musical inspiration. "At nineteen I bought a violin. I just walked into a shop and bought it because I dreamed about that sound," she recalled. "But then what do you do with a violin when you don't know how to play it?" She went on to learn a little, playing polkas and waltzes, picking up the music by ear. "I was playing a lot but not at a high level. I met Patrick because we were both playing folk music."

After Frandsen and Robin became a couple, Robin, always keen on becoming a violin maker, found a school in England that would accept him. In France, you could not be admitted into the official luthier schools unless you followed the system from junior high school. This has changed, but it had been a similar problem for Cauche, a member of perhaps the last generation for whom this impediment existed. In England, Robin began studies in violin making while Frandsen enrolled in the music school, both in the same building.

Frandsen said, "It was the cello that made me want to be a violin maker. I am a slow worker, and a cello takes two and a half times longer to make than a violin." A turning point came when Frandsen saw a cello being made. "When I saw how it was being done with the cello, it became a passion overnight. I wanted to make instruments. I tried very quickly after to make a violin at home."

She had had a bit of experience with woodworking in her youth, Frandsen said modestly. "In Danish schools you learn some practical things like cooking and a little of woodwork. I think I made a stupid chair." In England, she studied some of the greatest instruments under restoration, learned the art of luthiers to become a master herself, and nowadays serves as a judge for luthier school entries and for competitions.

Of the struggles and experiences women faced breaking into the male-dominated world of lutherie, Frandsen said, "Now for the schools it's changing. I jury for the national violin-making school at Mirecourt, and a few years back they took nine women and three men. It was exceptional, but now I think it is 50/50. But this is perhaps only the last ten years."

When I raised the issue of whether a woman's hands were strong enough for lutherie, Frandsen said dismissively, "That's just an idea, just an idea. When you watch a woman musician, you might ask how do you manage to press down those cello strings? I tried to play the cello, and it felt impossible at first. But it's training. I'm a normal person, but it's just training."

I asked Andrea why musicians have new instruments made for them, and she responded, "If you have confidence in the violin maker, that's a great advantage. You know the instrument is in good condition. With the old instruments, you don't know. Most old instruments have suffered from cracks, even if well restored. That's one thing. But the other thing is that you have an instrument that you can grow with."

Antoine Cauche, Jean-Louis Prochasson, and Andrea Frandsen all subscribed to Michaud's view that a new camaraderie had emerged among luthiers, an eagerness to share techniques and ideas and profit from them. What could be a better place for this exchange than the facilities at the Bois de lutherie, not far from Risoux forest, where Michaud can show instrument makers the perfect trees for violins, violas, and cellos?

A highly detailed topographical map of Risoux reveals the perimeter of the forest in thin red contour lines that are very tight, like wood grain, indicating an acute slope. Then they practically disappear through the entire middle area as the forest grows on an impressive plateau, exactly as Michaud described. Whereas the Paneveggio forest has a broad 5 to 6 percent slope with a three-thousand-foot differential in altitude, the Risoux forest flattens out at four thousand feet, an ideal altitude for tonewood-quality spruce. To the south, the forest plateau borders the lac du Joux, a clear natural lake that is also the largest one in Switzerland, at an altitude of over three thousand feet. The Orbe river feeds the lac du Joux from the west; after it exits the lake, it goes underground for three miles, reappearing in the town of Vallorbe. Along the valley a few miles into France, the Orbe river connects with lac des Rousses near its source. Despite the steep slope on the side of the plateau, riders on horseback use the switchback trails regularly, and one could easily imagine the pleasure of an equestrian tour of the forest garden.

Once on the plateau, similarities to the Paneveggio forest can be observed—namely, a moss- and lichen-covered rocky floor and a large variety of mushrooms, including some impressive pipe organ fungi. The Norway spruce roots constrict around rocks as if to consume them and the ground around them, yet the Risoux forest seems more open to both light and a greater variety of tree species than in the densest part of the Paneveggio.

While it takes decades of experience to understand how to read trees as Michaud does, even neophytes can find trees that are three or four feet in diameter, absolutely straight, and clean of former branches. Still, only a part of the tree, the lower trunk, suffices for instruments, and that is the part that tonewood businesses acquire from the contracted lumbering enterprises. Michaud—and other experts, for that matter—confess that ultimately they won't know if the wood they have purchased from the cutters is good enough for fine instruments until it is brought to the mill and the inner core is revealed. The selection process is like a combination of gambling and water divination, but years of experience and insider tips improve the odds.

Michaud gave a fitting description of Risoux as a forest garden, with well-maintained paths for machinery and stumps from trees that had either spatially impinged upon others or been selected for lumbering. Then again, there are no true wilderness areas or virgin forests of significant size left in Europe, and forests are progressively shrinking on many parts of the planet. During the eighteenth and nineteenth centuries, the demand for wood in Europe increased to such a degree that home woodlands and foreign forests were depleted to meet it. The leveling of the great white pine forests of the American Northeast for foreign and domestic exploitation is one example. As a commodity, white pine then was comparable in value to oil today.

Organized efforts to control or "tyrannize" nature have long been official policy in Europe. The extermination of wolves, brown bears, Eurasian lynx, and golden eagles was a part of this policy. Draining swamps to protect communities from mosquito-borne diseases and reclaiming land for farming or housing developments have become common practice. In *Tasting French Terroir,* Thomas Parker captures the seventeenth-century impulse to control and reshape nature when he describes Louis XIV's demand to build a Versailles vegetable garden on a swampy pond:

Even at the time, Versailles was such a well-known icon for its domination over nature that near contemporaries, such as Saint-Simon, were overly critical after the king's death, reporting that he did violence to Nature: "There it gave the king pleasure to tyrannize Nature and to tame her by expending art and money. . . ." Louis XIV, however, shocked his chief gardener, La Quintinie, by ordering his garden to be planned on the site commonly referred to as the *étang puant,* or "stinking pond."

In our epoch, we are keenly aware of the value and biological complexity of forests but nevertheless continue to destructively exploit them. If one element is changed, nature can respond in extraordinary ways. With the protections in place for the Parc naturel régional du Haut-Jura, the Eurasian lynx, with its spots and black ear tufts making it one of the most stunning of creatures, is making a comeback, along with sightings and evidence of wolves in the Massacre forest. Likewise, the golden eagle is coming back to areas such as the Paneveggio forest. The area protects the grand tétras, a wood grouse that populates Central Europe but has a tenuous foothold in France. It is the largest in the grouse family, and the lynx would delight in a resurgence. Wild boar rule throughout France and much of the world, and they leave their wild animal marks in European forests and cities. But many species of flora and fauna have vanished and will not return.

While Michaud may well be a tree whisperer, he is also an international entrepreneur and educator working with a network of luthiers. People who live in and with the forest are often romanticized. The Paneveggio has the poet-ranger Marcello Mazzucchi, who described the spruce columns as a natural cathedral. Risoux forest boasted its own tree whisperer, the celebrated forester Lorenzo Pellegrini. Pellegrini grew up in family-built huts and worked the forests around Abruzzo, cutting firewood and making clogs and tools. In a BBC interview with John Laurenson in 2013 he remarked, "I used to give my leftover polenta to the wolves." He settled in the Vallée de Joux and for fifty years worked on paths, cleared undergrowth, and selectively cut trees both for the wood industry and for the health of the forest. Master lumberjacks can fell a tree so precisely that it does not damage other vital trees around it. André Degon wrote of Pellegrini that "Lorenzo finds among 10,000 trees the one that will be exceptional. Like an old benevolent elf in the forest, he scrutinizes, feels the bark, looks, measures, caresses, and divines [tonewood]."

Pellegrini talked to trees with humble veneration, and at eighty would climb them to cut off deadwood to keep them healthy. He worked with the Swiss enterprise JMC Lutherie, created by Jean-Michel Capt and Céline Renard. While the focus of the company was originally on providing Jura tonewood for guitar tops, it also developed innovative tonewood designs for the Soundboard, a high-fidelity speaker made from carved spruce tonewood. Pellegrini cast a transforming spell on Capt and Renard and on those who interviewed him at the end of his life. Laurenson, while reporting on Pellegrini and Risoux for the BCC, could not resist the poetic coalescence of forest and music:

> [Wood] is always reacting to changes in temperature and humidity, always evolving. I listen to the crackle of the fire and the sound of cello strings making the wood sing. And think that I will never quite hear this music in the same way again. Because around here, when you hear an instrument like this, you think of the snow and the wind and the cuckoos and the bees in those tall violin trees.

La forêt du Massacre lies six miles south of the commune of Les Rousses, which is a station for both alpine and Nordic skiing. It has a different look and feel from Risoux, in part because of the topography. Whereas the perimeter of Risoux rises sharply to form a plateau at four thousand feet, the Massacre forest rises gradually to a five-thousand-foot ridge at le Crêt Pela. The gentle landscape features broad clearings, meadows, and trails that offer ideal paths for Nordic skiing. In the nonwinter months, the meadows provide pasture for the

Montbéliards, cows pied with reddish markings on white. They are the same superstar Jura cheese cows pastured in the Risoux forest area, but their meadows here are far more open and lusher.

Though the Massacre forest is sloped, it still offers the key conditions for tonewood-quality trees. These include a short growing season and the same limestone geological base and soil qualities, disposition to sunlight, and consistency of climate, including plenty of rain and snow. In the meadows, where the trees have more space, the branches extend nearly to the ground, and the full shape is what one might expect of a Christmas tree. This forest could hardly be lovelier under a snow cover, when it's possible to see how well adapted the trees are to winter conditions. When the weight of the snow becomes too much, the branches behave like a closing parasol, bowing to spill their burden. The bright sun streaming through the trees after the storm creates a dream world, rather than conjuring the slaughter of Italian mercenaries from which the forest acquired its name.

The tonewood spruce grows in tight stands with a high canopy, the density reducing the light. The trunks shed their lower branches, producing the desirable fifteen-foot clear-wood trunks. It does not take long to find those potential music wood groves, but identifying the ideal trees will always be a gamble. Future candidates are identified, and replacement trees are carefully fostered. A traveler passing through them to the top of the Massacre forest can see the Alps on the other side of Lake Geneva, including Mont Blanc, a peak that elicits the same sense of awe in contemporary viewers that it did among the poets of the Romantic era.

6

Rougemont, Switzerland

FORESTRY LAWS AND CHOOSING TONEWOOD SPRUCE

ON A GEMLIKE OCTOBER morning after night temperatures dip below freezing, the mountains and pastures of the Parc Naturel Régional Gruyère Pays-d'Enhaut are blanketed in sunlight between broad hoar-frost swaths of mountain shadows. The Swiss nature park covers 313 square miles, extending northwest of Montreux on Lake Geneva and including parts of the Fribourg and Vaudois Prealps. The park epitomizes a harmonious balance of nature with agriculture and lumbering, featuring peaks, river-carved valleys and gorges, chalet-dotted villages, ski lifts and trails, and contrasting patches of light green pastures and dark green conifer forests known as *forêts d'arolles*. Regional tourism invokes the French poet Baudelaire's refrain in *Invitation to the Voyage* to capture the atmosphere: "All is order there, and elegance, pleasure, peace and opulence." The Pays-d'Enhaut is not where you'd go for a roughing-it wilderness experience, but that doesn't rule out extremes: the Swiss love the outdoors, and some regularly test their skills and chance fate with mountain biking, sky diving, and rock climbing.

The limestone upfolds in the region resemble those in the Jura, although relatively recent glacial periods were an important factor in shaping the landscape. The surrounding peaks are considerably higher, some nearing seven thousand feet. Like the Jura, the Pays-d'Enhaut has a long cheese-making tradition. Piebald Holstein dairy cattle—both black and white and the less usual red and white—are treated as nearly sacred creatures since they are the source of Gruyère cheese. The villages celebrate *alpenage,* a parade of cows adorned with wildflower garlands, marking their autumn descent from mountain pastures. Could there be a more privileged place to be a cow?

Alpenhorns were used to call in the cows and to relay important communiqués across valleys, as they were throughout the Alps and the Carpathians. An alpenhorn is an eight- or nine-foot conical tube with a mouthpiece at one end and a curved bell at the other. Different tones are achieved through lip vibrations. They are crafted from the same Norway spruce tonewood used for violins. While the alpenhorn was originally designed to carry tonal messages for many miles, it is now used in festival players' groups, who perform even adaptations of Mozart. The Swiss also produced the büchel, a pinewood relative of the alphorn but with a wrapped tube more like a bugle, offering clear, higher tones and more musical agility.

Château d'Oex, located in the center of the Regional Park Gruyère Pays-d'Enhaut, is well known for its summer music festival, Bois qui Chante. The town becomes quieter in October, between the summer hiking and winter skiing seasons, though it has a devoted year-round population contributing to town life: church, schools, and competitive soccer under lights. Hoping to boost regional off-season activities, the town leaders conceived of a festival that would include lectures, cinema, symphonies, soloists, jazz, and children's ensembles. The name Bois qui Chante (wood that sings) honors the exceptional tonewood that comes from the Arses forest near Rougemont, only three miles away.

To enhance the festival spirit, organizers decorate Château d'Oex with chainsaw-carved sculptures of cellos and mushrooms that appear to sprout from a forest floor. The banners along the streets and a sculpture at the main village entry feature the music festival's logo:

half a cello—with a single f-hole—and half the distinctive silhouette of a spruce tree.

In 2018, I joined a group of sixteen hikers, strikingly diverse in age, gathered on the Place du Village to enjoy what was billed as "A Pleasure Walk in the Forest at Rougemont," which would include musical surprises and exhibits on woodworking professions. Organizers arrived in four-wheel-drive vehicles and took our group in the direction opposite Rougemont to Tine Station. A logging operation was under way in Rougemont, so this season's *balade* was detoured to the forêt de la Tine under the Dent de Corjon. A *dent,* or tooth, figuratively designates a sharp peak, and this one was an abiding presence through gaps in the spruce and pine branches.

Two experts—Robin Jousson, a luthier from Geneva, and Jean-Pierre Neff, president of the local groupement forestier—were on hand to teach us the fundamentals of tonewood acquisition and a bit about the legacy of forestry in the region. Jousson was a lean, attractive man in his thirties, with a combination of prematurely silver hair and dark eyebrows that both suited him and made him stand out. From an antique wooden case, he extracted an unfinished violin that looked ghostlike. "This instrument was made in Romania in a very large workshop, fifty workers, a kind of assembly line," he explained. "The violin is entirely correct with an interior that is a little rough, but I intend to smooth it out. This process of sending instruments that are manufactured in one place but need correcting and finishing in another workshop is common. The work includes applying stain and varnish and fitting it with pegs, bridge, and strings. An etiquette identifying the manufacturer is glued inside under an f-hole where it can be seen. When finished, this will fall in the category of a study or beginner's level instrument."

He lifted off the carved belly with its bass bar glued lengthwise in place. A bass bar is an oblong strip of spruce that runs from the neck past the f-holes to the bottom to offer structural support against the

Luthier Robin Jousson in the Swiss forêt de la Tine under the Dent de Corjon, explaining which trees provide the best tonewood for violins.

tension of the strings. Jousson pointed out that the two parts were machined from quality spruce similar to that found in the Arses forest. The neck, back, and sides were made from the traditional figured maple found in the Carpathians.

With Balkan maple, Jousson said, "Individual trees with figuring sometimes grew large enough to provide wood for double bass backs and sides. It is the type of tree one finds in a primeval forest, not here."

Rougemont, Switzerland

75

This begs the question of how Balkan tree cutters gain access to such precious trees. Were there fewer legal restrictions on lumbering in the forests?

Jousson directed attention to the spruce in the forêt de la Tine. He ticked off the requisite qualities for high-end tonewood—elasticity, lightness, and homogeneity of grain—and singled out trees that would have tonewood potential ten or twenty years in the future. He emphasized the importance of clear wood coming from the lower part of spruce trees that grow in dense proximity to each other at four thousand feet. The lower branches are shed very early in favor of crowns that reach upward into the sunlight. While particular anomalies in maple grain are highly valued for aesthetic reasons, clear wood in spruce is key for quality resonance. Knots, defects, and twisting distortions in the grain are strictly avoided for the quartet instruments. Guitars have become an exception, with some luthiers starting to appreciate bear claw figuring in spruce tops. Indeed, some musicians and luthiers believe bear claw spruce is stiffer and thus more suited to flatpicking instruments than straight grain wood.

"We look for spruce trees that have lost their lower branches as early as possible during their growth," Jousson continued. "Branches mean knots run deep in the wood. We cut twin billets from flawless wood." Speculatively, he held up the violin top to a spruce, saying that its diameter might be sufficient for a violin. "We face the same problem with maples. We must find a very rare maple tree, one not only with figuring but also with a diameter large enough to make backs for violas, cellos, or possibly double basses. For a cello, a tree must be close to three feet in diameter. For a bass, four feet. Such spruce trees can be found in the Pays-d'Enhaut, but not many in this forest. It is necessary to go to the Arses forest above Rougemont to find large trees with a homogenous grain."

In areas where chalets are prevalent, knotty pine is considered desirable as interior paneling for the cozy alpine look it imparts. However, the wood is not strong or durable, and in an instrument, it would inter-fere with resonance. With little evidence of branches on a trunk, it is often hard to tell exactly what the structure of the interior might be like. To illustrate how deep the knots run, Jousson pulled out a newspaper cutout showing a photograph of a log sculpted by Giuseppe Penone, part of his "Hidden Life Within" project. The photograph showed an enormous log with areas chopped out of the interior. The growth layers were then carefully carved away to reveal the nascent tree, perhaps a twenty-year-old sapling, preserved within the heartwood. Art aside, the photography clearly illustrated Jousson's point that inner branch structures can permeate the heartwood, causing buckling or waves in the grain. Jousson held up his Romanian violin top and turned it at angles against a potential Swiss tonewood spruce trunk, along with a billet to demonstrate the quarter cut and the twin split to create a symmetry of wood grain. He wanted to emphasize how rare are trees that offer unblemished wood.

Jean-Pierre Neff followed Jousson's talk. Neff is a forestry engi-neer and a technical expert who served as president of the Groupe-ment forestier du Pays-d'Enhaut (GFPE) et syndic de Rossinière. He engages directly with lumbering enterprises to ensure that the goals of the forest code and the Direction Générale de l'environnement are respected. Neff probably knew the Pays-d'Enhaut more intimately than almost anyone, and was strongly committed to preserving it. For us, he briefly outlined the history of forest exploitation in the Château d'Oex area—one that comprises the community of Rossinière and the forests of Brochet and Sauta, a communal parcel of several hundred hectares.

"Lumbering has played a central role in this area since the eigh-teenth and nineteenth centuries," he began, "providing wood not only for Swiss communities but also for an enormous wood exportation de-mand. The logs had impressive value at the time. Ironworks foundries also required a large supply of wood. In the Rossinière region, the train line did not arrive until 1924, so wood was transported by flotation in the Sarine river. Logs were floated a hundred miles to large commercial milling operations. Rossinière also supported three sawmills, taking advantage of the Sarine and a nearby brook as power sources."

Though only eighty miles long, the Sarine was an important commercial river, winding through the city of Fribourg before joining the Aare, a tributary of the Rhine. The *flottage* of wood in the Pays d'Enhaut mirrored the method used in the Val di Fiemme with the Avisio river and its communication with the Adige, followed by transport on the Po.

Neff enumerated a few local distinctions in forest management. "The forests around Rossinière belonged to the commune in the eighteenth century," he said, "whereas in Rougemont, with its chateau, the forest had been in part privately owned. Members of the commune of Rossinière became the beneficiaries of lumber sales, and the profits were used to pay their tax bills."

All was not easy for the inhabitants, however. Catastrophes led to one of the most important laws in European forestry. Because forests experienced heavy damage from rockfalls, mudslides, and wind snapping in storms that affected production, in the late eighteenth century, codes were formulated, first for Bâle by Bishop Joseph William, in 1755, followed in 1760 by scientific communities in Zurich and Bern. The early teaching of forestry and initiatives enforcing forest restoration led to the establishment in 1876 of the first federal forest act. In each generation, inhabitants had the right to cut and sell wood during their life span as long as they did not destroy the vitality of the forests. The forest must be able to regenerate to serve as a durable community resource for the future, including periods of adversity.

To protect the forests, associations for forestry, such as the Groupement forestier du Pays-d'Enhaut, were created to impose an established code. France supports its own groupement forestier, its code stating, "The purpose of forest groupings is the establishment, improvement, equipping, conservation or management of one or more forest areas, and generally any operations that may be attached to or derive from this object, provided that such operations do not alter the civil character of the group."

Neff spoke of other lumbering developments in the Rossinière area. "The flotation of logs caused damage to the river and land along its banks. Protests arose, provoking more protective laws that effectively would end flotation on the Sarine. Dams followed, providing hydro-electricity and leading to the modernization of sawmills. At the same time, lumber depots became numerous and convenient. Yet with all of these developments, the value of wood remained the same over fifty years, while the cost of labor increased enormously, making wood exploitation unprofitable. Lumbering businesses had to put on the brakes unless they received subsidies."

Neff felt that some sectors were too well served by machines, and the effect was similar to that which could be seen in Italy and the Jura. The character of a forest is materially changed by these machines. With numerous stumps in open spaces between trees, the look is one of amputation, with lumbering access roads snaking through all.

Neff's specialty being forestry, he generally left the discussion of musical instrument wood to Jousson, but he did draw a striking parallel between tonewood and *bois tavaillon*. *Tavaillons* are shakes used for roofing or façades in mountain areas, such as the Swiss Romande, the Jura, the volcanic mountains of the Massif Central, and the Pyrenees. The wood that gives voice to the world's best instruments shares some characteristics with the extremely durable wood shingling capable of lasting four hundred years or more on chalets. In fact, some sophisticated counterfeits of historical instruments were likely made from recovered Norway spruce chalet beams.

The woodcrafter who makes these shakes is a specialist known as a *tavailloneur*. His primary tool is a shingle froe—a downward-aimed blade with a handle on one end that makes it L-shaped. Placing the sharp edge carefully along the cross-cut grain of a log and giving it a well-aimed whack with a mallet, the experienced *tavailloneur* can cleave off fairly precise half-inch-thick shingles. Specially selected and

Rougemont, Switzerland

aged spruce has become mythic for its longevity as a building material for the old Swiss chalets, even as it is treasured for its acoustical properties in instrument making.

Neff said, "For *tavaillons* and *bois de resonance,* we look in the same sectors at the right altitude where there is not a lot of wind that could interfere with straight tree growth. There are many sayings, superstitions, and traditions for acquiring good wood. It has to be cut in the right season, at the right phase of the moon, and at the right hour. Professor Zücher conducted a ten-year study to prove scientifically the traditional myth that cutting during the new moon in winter ensures wood quality."

Ernst Zücher has produced numerous studies on the influence of the lunar cycle on planting and harvesting traditions. He is charismatic in documentaries, and his writing appealingly interweaves classical ideas, anthropology, and botany. In his essay "Plants and the Moon: Traditions and Phenomena," Zücher outlines some of his anthropological findings:

On perusing works about folk customs and country lore, or reading the accounts of ancient authors (such as Hesiod, an 8th century B.C. Greek poet, author of *Works and Days*), or again when talking with gardeners, small farmers, woodcutters, or those working with wood about their empirical experience, one is led unerringly to 2 observations:

- In addition to the rhythm of the seasons, solar in nature from a geocentric point of view, these sources and these people systematically evoke the lunar cycles as a factor influencing the growth, the structures and certain properties of plants;
- Despite the geographical distance between the informants, there are often similarities among the declarations concerning this factor.

He goes on to say that

> all these traditions seem to be based on similar observations, for
> example, the period of the new moon (or waning moon) is considered
> the most favorable for felling trees to give durable wood for
> construction, resistant to insects and fungi.

This passage echoes Theophrastus, who stated in the third century BCE that "wood cut when the moon decreases is harder and less susceptible to mold." Zücher argues that the waning moon lowers the hygroscopic levels in wood through gravitational pull on "free water," water not bound within the cells of wood. Plenty of experts remain skeptical, and it was difficult to judge what Neff believed, even though he cited an experiment in which Zücher compared the absorption of ink in cores of moonwood and non-moonwood, the former resisting ink and the latter sucking it up.

The idea of moonwood in a musical instrument holds great imaginative appeal, invoking the ancient lunar timetable for harvesting trees. Tonewood Switzerland, located in the southeastern canton of Graubünden, features moonwood billets while touting Zücher's experiments. As with Michaud's Bois de lutherie operation, each log here is identified, and each billet carries a brand with a record of its level of quality and harvesting date. The billets also feature a small black thumbnail moon, mark of a lunar cycle–based harvest.

In light of Neff's remark that the numerous stumps around logging roads looked like amputations, Zücher's research into tree regeneration probably interested him far more than lunar harvesting, in that it reveals the complex communication between trees and the role such communication plays in forest regeneration. Certain types of tree trunks, those of maples in particular, possess the ability to send up new shoots though their own root systems intermingled and possibly anastomosed, through natural root grafting, with those of neighboring trees. Survival of the fittest sometimes depends on extensive underground cooperation and networking.

Neff emphasized that only a very small percentage of the wood produced by the forests is of sufficient quality for instrument making and *tavaillons,* and even then a trial-and-error approach is required. Milling suppliers notify luthiers when a likely tree is found, and they take only a small section of it. Other parts of the tree might be used for wood shakes, construction, or restoration work.

"The wood possesses its own aesthetic allure," Neff commented, "and it is expensive. The lower-quality wood requires preservative treatments and painting. The really good wood is like a fossil in the elements: nothing will affect it."

One hiker asked, "So why do they varnish a violin?" Knowing well the multipurpose necessity of instrument varnish and finishing, Jean-Pierre answered, trying to conceal his amusement, "The violin is more like a piece of furniture."

We gathered around a stump that stood nearly two feet high. Jousson waited patiently before announcing one of the surprises of the tour: a contest to count the year rings and calculate the age of the large Norway spruce that had been cut down a few years earlier. The children and adults would compete separately for different sorts of prizes, products of the forest selected to please each age group and keep answers in perspective. The exercise emphasized the importance of tree rings, slow growth, the tight pattern, trees nearly two hundred years old. Most luthiers purchase wood from specialty milling enterprises, but Jousson acquires wood from Rougemont. "I buy portions of logs directly and prepare the billets myself."

There is something about the air and space in the mountains that makes scenes look simultaneously vivid and dreamy; distances appear compressed. The slopes are layered with darkening pastures, then a conifer forest with a few yellow spots of October deciduous trees, and limestone peaks rising over tree lines and the shadows of other ridges. The evening radiance of the Dolomites in Italy is unmistakable: alpenglow. The rock peaks around Château d'Oex produce their own luminous stone.

The Arses forest above Rougemont is where older trees can be found, thanks in part to conservation by private owners, in contrast to communal associations, which, as in Rossinière, profit from more extensive logging. During the eleventh century, the Count of Gruyère granted to an order of monks from Cluny in Bourgogne the right to establish a priory on the undeveloped area. A small Romanesque church duly followed, as did the first and only Vaud convent. The priory has been reconstructed, as has the meticulously maintained walled Château de Rougemont, featuring green-and-white-striped shutters and two small towers. Pastures completely surround the chateau. While inhabitants can gaze on Holsteins grazing in the pasture by the river, they can also peer up at La Vidémanette in the Gstaad Dolomites and the spread of the Arses forest.

The Sarine river runs through Rougemont near the chateau and the église Saint-Nicolas with its surrounding cemetery. Just to the right is the gondola lift station for the Vidémanette; on the left, a stack of enormous spruce logs. Le Revers, a paved road to a few residences, transforms into a crushed stone forestry road. A steeper path leads into the Arses forest, where, at first, I saw areas of colorful mixed autumn trees—beech, oak, and maples—interspersed with pockets of pine and spruce. But above four thousand feet and past the last pasture, the mixed woods give way to stands of gigantic spruce. The tightly packed trees have acquired the look of pillars, branchless for eighty feet or more, prime quality timber. The experts would determine whether their trees had violins and cellos in them, or seemingly eternal chalets with *tavaillons* that will weather gray and brown.

In the Arses forest on a steep, rocky slope with stumps of recently cut trees and storm-splintered trunks, the foresters planted spruce saplings in deer-resistant caging. It will take a minimum of one hundred and fifty years for the trees to mature enough for violin wood, and then a very determined luthier in the twenty-second century, celebrating five hundred years of Stradivarius instruments, will get to work.

7

Styria, Austria, and Transylvania

TONEWOOD SOURCES AND ENVIRONMENTAL ISSUES

VIENNA IS ONE OF Europe's great historic centers for classical music, thanks in large part to the Habsburg family's patronage. In fact, over the centuries, members of the Habsburg family became composers and performers themselves. Because of Vienna's artistic vitality, Haydn, Mozart, and Beethoven lived and composed in the city, which in turn improved their fortunes. Schubert and Strauss were born in Vienna, and Mahler graduated from the Vienna Conservatory and was appointed director of the Vienna Court Opera. In response to the boom in composition and performance, luthiers and other instrument makers flourished in Vienna, responding innovatively to the new demands of larger venues and greater compositional complexity. While the organ served churches and the harpsichord found its place in large rooms, the fortepiano—a term meaning "loud-soft"—could be heard in halls and was the early piano on which Haydn, Mozart, and the young Beethoven composed many of their works, allowing greater range and, as the name suggests, more nuanced sound.

The fortepiano—in which a leather-covered hammer device strikes the strings, as opposed to the plucking mechanism employed by the harpsichord—was an invention of the Italian Bartolomeo Cristofori at the turn of the eighteenth century. Exceptional specimens were also produced by Viennese instrument makers. One of the most famous of these was Anton Walter, who held the title of imperial royal chamber organ builder and instrument maker. Mozart composed during his most productive periods on a Walter instrument. The progress of developments over the next two centuries led to the construction of massive grand pianos by Bösendorfer—instruments that boasted ninety-two and even ninety-seven keys rather than the standard eighty-eight, which helped with transposing organ music to piano. (The full name of pianos as we know them today, pianoforte, is an inversion of the term "fortepiano." The piano succeeded the fortepiano after about 1830.)

Salzburg is also considered one of the world's most important music centers, in part because it was Mozart's birthplace. The city is home to

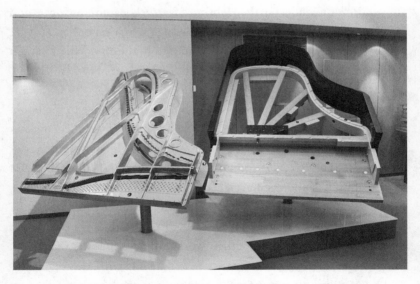

Cast-iron frame, soundboard, and cabinet of a piano in the Berlin Musical Instrument Museum.

the University Mozarteum, dedicated to studies in the arts and music, and also hosts the internationally known Salzburg music festivals, one in spring and the other in summer. The Salzburg Museum displays a large array of musical instruments, giving a historical overview of wind, string, plucked, and percussion instruments, along with the keyboard instruments—organs, harpsichords, and fortepianos. The museum boasts several oddities: the steel piano, a nail violin, and the glockenspiel, which Mozart dubbed the "steel laughter" instrument for Papageno's role in the *Magic Flute*. Finally, the city was the setting for the first part of Maria von Trapp's memoir *The Story of the Trapp Family Singers,* which inspired the musical *The Sound of Music* and, subsequently, the film starring Julie Andrews and Christopher Plummer.

It is little wonder that Jean-Marie Ballu would name Salzburg a principal tonewood location in his book *Bois de musique*. Bavaria, with its rich instrument-making traditions and the Ore Mountains, lies to the north of Salzburg, and the Austrian Alps rise to the south, providing both Vienna's and Salzburg's luthiers and instrument makers with top-quality spruce tonewood. Maple, too, can be easily accessed from the Balkans.

The mountainous Austrian state of Styria, 75 percent of which is carpeted with forests, runs south of Salzburg and Vienna to the Slovenia border. In the Styrian town of Mariazell, Dr. Reinhard Zach worked for decades as a local general practitioner while also becoming the unlikely founder of the milling enterprise Traditional Tonewood. Mariazell is on the southern end of the Ötscher-Tormäuer Nature Park and a sizable portion of so-called virgin forest near Dürrenstein. Even Traditional Tonewood's business office seemed unusual: a small desk in a shop called Heavenly Gifts for All Seasons, just behind Mariazell's storied Basilica Mariä Geburt, Austria's most notable religious pilgrimage attraction. Zach thus took orders for quartet instrument and guitar tonewood amid postcards, figurines, table trinkets, and Christmas ornaments, often embellished with hearts. He recently retired from his practice and lives mainly in Vienna, only a hundred miles away. However, he just could not relinquish his tonewood business. Working with wood became an obsession for the town doctor, as did the region's mountain forests, which he continued to research. When I first spoke to Zach on his own office phone in the gift shop, he labeled the region. "We call it the Austrian outback."

Many spruce forests that supply tonewood are located near ski resorts, and one might easily imagine Zach spending forty years mending broken bones, sprained muscles, and damaged joints; but on the contrary, he encountered an ample number of maladies in Mariazell to keep him professionally busy. It was tonewood that drew him to the forests. "I stopped working as a physician, but I can't stay away from the wood, much as I might try," he said ruefully. "It's a passion. I'll probably work with wood for the rest of my life." This hobby now requires a two-hour commute from Vienna to Mariazell, as well as business trips to see loggers and suppliers, often in Slovenia. He also travels frequently to international musical instrument festivals, where he displays his products.

Explaining how his passion for tonewood started, Zach recalled, "I played the violin, and while I was in medical school in Graz, I had the idea that I could own a high-quality violin for little money if I found an old one in need of restoration. I bought a broken-down violin in a pawn shop and then went to the library and took out a manual on lutherie. It turned out to be so technical that I couldn't understand any of it at first. Still, I restored the violin and then turned to making them from scratch myself. I ended up making ten violins and two violas."

His interest shifted from working as an amateur luthier to finding, processing, and stocking music wood. "I would see beautiful old spruce trees being cut around Mariazell and thought they might provide excellent violin tops. It turns out that I was right. But it isn't easy to find just the right old trees without defects. Primal forest still exists in Rothwald near Dürrenstein mountain just west of Mariazell. Somehow Rothwald managed to survive the pervasive exploitation of ironworks, and now the forest is protected as it should be." Charcoal was used in massive quantities for a variety of purposes during the Industrial Revolution, including smelting, leading to deforestation in many northern European regions, including Austria.

Zach was well informed on and greatly disturbed by the problems afflicting Austrian spruce forests, the most alarming being climate change. Norway spruce has a relatively shallow root system, giving the tree an advantage in rocky environments but also exposing its Achilles heel: an inability to tap into deep water sources, which heightens the threat to these trees in heat and drought. Rising temperatures have also hastened the spread of the pine bark beetle, both in altitude and across territory. Bark beetle outbreaks are occurring in North America, parts of Siberia, and Europe. The Czech Republic, Poland, Germany, and Slovakia have experienced particularly destructive attacks. Other species damage spruce as well, including *Heterobasidion annosum,* which causes root rot, and *Armillaria* fungi, which attack weakened trees. Zach's worries for the Austrian forests were justified. It may turn out that in parts of Europe only stands of Norway spruce at higher altitudes will survive the effects of climate change.

The Traditional Tonewood Company milled and stocked its billets in Halltal, a hamlet just outside Mariazell on the Salza river. The Salza is a significant feeder for a hydroelectric reservoir, and also supplies water to Vienna. While peaks like the Dürrenstein and Ötscher were formed from the same upthrust limestone as the Dolomites, the Jura, and the Gruyère region, the water in the rivers and lakes is crystalline, evincing neither silt nor the milky green color of rivers fed by glaciers. The mountains show no tree lines since even the tallest trees reach an altitude of less than six thousand feet. Nevertheless, the elevation of many of the slopes exceeds four thousand feet, making them ideal sites for large, slow-growing spruce. While there is some extant primeval forest, the more significant forest areas have enjoyed a reprieve from cutting, allowing some trees to reach ages of up to two hundred years.

Zach partnered with Hermann Ofner, who ran a furniture-making and restoration workshop on the ground level of a two-story shed stocked with billets and machinery for processing logs. The Traditional Tonewood showroom, which includes a small art gallery, stands close to the main road, and the Ofner family lives in a neighboring building with deep red shingles, orange structural beams, and green trim around the window frames. Such colorful buildings add to Mariazell's appealing character. On the shed's second floor, dedicated to tonewood stock, figured maple that had been set out near a window possessed some of the most striking chatoyance effects seen in billets. Fine outlines of violins and violas had been traced on them in pencil. Some pieces of attractive wood were large enough for single-piece backs, seen often in the antique stringed instruments. Maple appeared to be one of Traditional Tonewood's specialties, probably because Styria was so close to Slovenia, known to have large maples.

Figured maple billets, Traditional Tonewood, Mariazell, Austria.

Though most prevalent, spruce and maple were not the only types of wood on the premises. A large matching pair of cherry billets was destined to become the back for a double bass. As beautiful as this pair was, the poplar set next to them would likely provide better resonance. The challenge of finding and milling such large pieces of wood—flawless, and a minimum of four feet in diameter—is considerable, just as Jousson had explained. A superior quality pair of billets for a double bass might easily sell for $1,000. Zach also sold rippled pearwood and poplar violin backs for experiment-minded luthiers bucking tradition. Pearwood tends to be denser and thus heavier than maple, and may not have as impressive an "attack" (the speed of note perception in tonewood), but it is appreciated for its broad sound and harmonics.

Zach had methodically organized and identified billets on steel rack shelves that stood in rows. Visiting the site, I had the impression of walking among the stacks of an old library, but instead of books I browsed Gemini matching twin wedges, backs and tops coming from different types of wood. The shelves held larger wedges of curly maple, partially split, waiting for finer cuts yet already distinctly showing the elegant wavy growth pattern.

The relationship between the doctor and the carpenter and his family was clearly a warm one. The Ofner children grew up in this seemingly idyllic spot and had crafted wonderfully detailed, playfully ghoulish masks that were on display with Ofner's furniture. Lutherie and furniture making require similar skills and instincts. In fact, many luthiers start out in furniture making and restoration. Both crafts involve a passion for wood textures and grain patterns, pliability, odor, and, in the case of the luthier, resonance. Those who work with wood love to sculpt it, and invariably their gifts are enhanced with training.

Rothwald forest, on the outskirts of Mariazell, is a strictly protected nature reserve. It is included in the Dürrenstein Wilderness Area, established in 2002. Publicity brochures for the reserve claim that "the primeval forest Rothwald is the largest remaining primeval forest in Central Europe. This area has remained untouched by axe or chainsaw since the last ice age." The forests surrounding Rothwald, though exploited in the past, now also fall within protected zones and are gradually returning to a wild state. Dürrenstein Wilderness Area occupies itself with forest research, and conservators maintain a meticulous inventory of plants and animals. Dürrenstein researchers assert that Rothwald supports six hundred species of fungi. Among the animal denizens are the Ural owl and the white-backed woodpecker, four types of grouse, red deer, chamois, alpine hare, and even the brown bear, exterminated in much of Europe.

The story behind the forest is a little more complicated. Albert von Rothschild, a nineteenth-century Austrian banker and railroad mogul, became a philanthropist and major property owner. In 1875, he bought Rothwald forest. Previously a monastery in Gaming had managed the forest until Josef II expropriated it as a part of Habsburg lands. Over a ninety-year period, some of the primeval forest was exploited. However, Rothwald forest managed to remain untouched, thanks to the difficulty in accessing the terrain and issues regarding political boundaries and exploitation quarrels. Rothschild, passionate about nature, preserved the forest in its primeval state. Recently nature conservation legislation was enacted, and the land became protected by the state.

Rothwald seems to support more beech, maple, ash, and elm than can be found in the Paneveggio, Risoux, and Arses forests. In mixed woodland such as this, visitors can marvel at beech trees in full October color. However, at higher altitudes, the soil becomes rockier and pines and spruce begin to dominate. The surrounding area is much less developed in terms of visible communes, roads, and agriculture—thus the "Austrian Outback" notion.

Tonewood milling companies are mostly very small commercial enterprises, selling on the internet, at festivals, and through direct visits from luthiers. Zach's enterprise is smaller than most, and yet he still sells his tonewood both locally and internationally. As a doctor, music lover, amateur musician, and woodworker, he has provided excellent instrument wood by following his own instincts about the forests he has lived among his whole professional life.

Austria and much of Western Europe have enacted rigorous controls on lumbering, forcing local furniture and construction companies to seek outside sources of wood. A combination of corruption and lax forest policy in former Soviet satellite countries—including Poland, Romania, Slovenia, Slovakia, and Bosnia-Herzegovina—has allowed foreign companies to exploit their forest resources. The instrument-making industry uses very rare and specific sorts of wood in relatively small quantities and must work with larger logging operations to acquire materials. (Bernard Michaud obtained wood from Romania, as do contemporary tonewood enterprises such as Drewbas Tonewood in Poland, Toneholz in Germany, and Maderas Barber in Spain.)

Romania has its own tonewood mills, and one of the best known is Carpathian Tonewood in Râşnov. The drive across Romania to Râşnov winds through a variety of mountain areas, including Apuseni Natural Park and the Făgăraş Mountains, all a part of the Carpathian chain, and the plains of the Transylvanian Basin, which occupy the center of the country. Râşnov lies just south of the town of Braşov, surrounded by the Eastern Carpathian Mountains.

The area is known for a nongovernmental organization project called the Millions of Friends Association, an enormous animal protection sanctuary serving a broad spectrum of species with veterinary help, rehabilitation, home placement, and reintroduction programs. One of its more impressive projects is the liBearty Bear Sanctuary, where brown bears are rehabilitated from captivity on lush forested land. Brown bears, wolves, and the Eurasian lynx, the national animal, still roam secluded areas in the Carpathian forests. Romania holds some of the last remaining primeval forest in Europe, and Braşov county contains potentially the largest in the country, at 49,601 hectares.

Carpathian Tonewood is situated in an industrial zone with an impressive view of the thirteenth-century Râșnov Citadel. The industrial zone offers no street numbers and includes a lumbering enterprise for construction materials: even some local workers were unaware of Carpathian Tonewood, or of where 25 Garii Street might be located. However, a white cement building topped with corrugated steel roofing offered a clue: smaller open sheds in the yard with racks for aging wood. When I queried an athletic-looking woman wearing a black stocking cap about the company, she confirmed that it was Carpathian Tonewood. She pulled out her portable phone and called Mihai Filip, the company's quality control and marketing officer.

Within five minutes, Filip pulled up in a small car and was immediately charming, apologizing that the owner, Catalin Murgoci, was away in China participating in an exhibition. Being unnecessarily modest, he also apologized for his English. Clad in a dark green safari jacket over a green flannel shirt open to show a red t-shirt underneath—practical layering for the October mountains—Filip was hard to place agewise, but he appeared youthful and energetic.

I was curious about how Filip had started working for Carpathian Tonewood. "I live here, in this town," he responded. "The business was here, and my family and Catalin, the owner, were friends. He noticed that I played guitar, and he said, 'You know, I'm making parts for guitars. You should come and take a look at them.' I came once, twice, and then regularly, and he said, 'Maybe you would like to work here.'"

When I asked Filip how he had learned his trade, he confessed that he had had no formal forestry training, but told me that the forest had been a crucial part of his life.

"It's true, I didn't go to forestry school. But since I was a little child, I lived in the country, and we went into the forest to cut wood for timber and firewood. So this is natural to us. And we took long walks, and we still do, through the woods with children, family, and friends. This is our main hobby on the weekends or when we can take a break. This time of year is fantastic."

Mihai Filip at Carpathian Tonewood in Râșnov, Romania.

Filip possessed more than a deep affinity for the local forest; he possessed a good ear for identifying top-quality tonewood.

"My particular job here is quality control," he went on. "I tap the wood and try to distinguish between different trees, different species, and how the tone resonates—the longer, the deeper, the lower, or the highest. I played guitar for fifteen years and recently took up violin. It's all in the ear, it's finesse. The ear becomes refined."

Filip suggested that sensibilities can be chiseled like the instrument itself—a metaphor that has become common among foresters, luthiers, and musicians. He was trying his hand at making a guitar and had already built the front and back, and was using a bending iron to shape the sides. Gluing the sides to the back and the front would be the next step. He was also in the midst of fashioning a violin, his new passion.

While there are certain objective criteria by which tonewood is chosen, personal instincts or subjective considerations play a substantial role. "For a tree to look like a good candidate, it has to be without knots," Filip commented. "This is easier to see when we debark it. The grain also has to be straight." Many factors, such as wind or growing disposition, can lead to twists in spruce that may not be easily detected in the standing tree. "Only when we open a log can we see if we have the right wood. It's a long process—there are many risks, starting from buying and going through cutting. You could cut right into the best part, and, when you split it, you might discover a knot there. But also you might be lucky. You might cut through the knot and find that you can still use the best parts. There have been more than a few nights that I didn't sleep because of the big investment, and I would become anxious until the next day when we open it and see how it is. Is it right or not? Usually 50 percent right and 50 percent wrong. It's a gamble."

Filip went on to describe how Carpathian Tonewood evolved. "It started as a different kind of company," he said, "and Catalin was working with them. They built houses until 2004. They began seeing that the quality of the wood was too good for simply making boards. They said we might try processing tonewood. Little by little, the company changed and the interests split. The ones who made houses moved, while Catalin stayed here with tonewood production. Until four or five years ago, we only supplied wood to the musical instrument factories. But then we started to make the finished product, a little more refined so that we can sell it to luthiers, who demanded better quality."

He added, "We are now in the time period when we take a pause, because the time to cut the trees we consider best runs from November until March. The moisture in the trees is lower during those months. We go to the different sites in this part of the country and in the north, near Reghin and Bistrița, even as far as Moldavia.

"We have people in certain places who call to say we have found you a candidate, or two or five—big maples or spruce, or poplar. They don't cut into the tree to mark it because the water gets into the wound and it stains, blackens the wood, so they use a colored marker. We go and we check them out, and if we think they are a good investment, we buy them. It's like betting on the percentage. There are several transporters for logs. We call them, and they drive to different places and fill a truck before they come here and stack our small number of logs."

Inside the cement building on the right, a large horizontal band saw milling machine lay dormant within a yellow steel frame designed to support the saw as it cut through large-diameter logs. The frame moved on its own set of rails so that the saw would pass through the length of log.

"With this first cut," Filip said, "we split a big log, maybe three feet in diameter. Because it is long and thick, we must use finesse cutting, adjusting the blade so that it doesn't vibrate. The vibration occurs when the blade comes to a knot. To avoid loss during the main cut, we can change the direction of the blade. The knots are a fault and leave a gap in the grain. They are absolutely no good—not for acoustics or for structural integrity since they leave holes. You can't have knots in the pattern. Even when they are outside the pattern, they still influence the quality of the billet by bending the fiber."

The moment at which the longitudinal cut is made turns out to be decisive, revealing the result of Filip and Catalin's gamble. "We inspect the cut log and then we make a decision," Filip explained. "How should we cut it? We decide in this order. Is it good for a double bass, is it good for cellos, is this good for archtop guitars, jazz guitars, or just guitars? Last are violins. Only small pieces are needed, but they are still the most important because of the quality they require. We try to make all cuttings regular, perpendicular to the rings of a tree. Then we take them outside to dry."

Throughout this narrative, Filip underscored at several points the constant risks involved in working with tonewood. "When the wood leaves this company and a luthier tries to model it, carve it, sculpt it, he may still find flaws, defects in the wood. It's a gamble from when you say 'this tree will go down' until it becomes the varnished instrument."

When one discusses sources of wood with luthiers and tonewood distributors, invariably the Balkan countries are mentioned. Even in the seventeenth century, wood was making its way from the Balkans to Italy. When I asked if spruce and maple from the Balkans had superior qualities, Filip shrugged. "I don't have much to compare it with," he responded. "Luthiers have wood from all around the world. I have heard that maple from Romania is softer and easier to carve, and the stone wood, the spruce, is just exceptional. I have not seen Sitka or anyone else's spruce. My particular job here is to grade quality. We grade in categories. The lowest is B, then one A. AA is better, AAA is even better, and the best is master grade. That's very rare, though. I would say we come across it once in three years. I don't know precisely how much wood we cut, maybe around sixty cubic meters, fifty to a hundred logs a year. One in three hundred would be a master."

While we walk through the stacks of stocked wood, Filip points out good and poor qualities of different billets and what instrument they are destined to become. One piece of maple for a violin is a little bit bent and the flames are not pronounced, so it is rated A. He notes some high-quality violin tops, then moves to a particular stack in the back of the inventory. "Parts that don't match for a classical guitar or for a western guitar, a smaller piece like this, we use for a fado, which is a very popular instrument here, something like a banjo."

He was referring to the Portuguese guitar, which is really more like a tenor mandolin or a Spanish bandurria than a banjo. Fado is a genre of passionate and mournful Portuguese music born in the early nineteenth century in the taverns and on the docks of Lisbon. The instrument that shares the name fado has six pairs of strings and uses a fan-shaped Preston tuner, also called a watchkey tuner.

We spent a leisurely time among the stock, looking at parts for a double bass, more guitars, and some cellos. "We have some cello backs here, but not the best quality. The best quality I will show last." Filip paused for a moment, gathering his thoughts. "You know, grading is a funny thing. If you get too much good wood, you tend to grade it more critically, lowering an AA to an A. If you've only seen bad pieces and you see a little good, then you say 'wow.' Then if the next year when you see it is all exquisite, you would rethink your grading." He held up a striking piece of tonewood and turned it over and over appreciatively. "This is a poplar with a wave figure in it. We sold it on the first day we put it on the website. It's clean, very clean. You very rarely encounter this. The flames are not as obvious as I would have liked, but this kind of tree we find maybe once in ten years, straight and no defects. It's from 2016. The billets sold for $1,200. So when you split a log in the morning, you say, 'Oh, my God, this is a nightmare.' Or 'Oh God, perfect, billets for five double basses!'"

The quality of the poplar for the double bass was unquestionable, as was much of the prime stock kept near to the Carpathian Tonewood sales office. As Filip scanned the reserved maple stock intended for use in crafting steel-stringed guitars, he explained that many of the best pieces that were advertised had already sold. Nevertheless, he slid from the shelves three sets destined to become maple guitar backs, all graded AAA. With another, he exclaimed, "It's a master, spotless." The chatoyancy was pronounced.

He brought this set down to the machine room to demonstrate cutting the sides. "Luthiers have plans and know how wide they want the sides to be. We sell these pieces usually from four and a quarter to five inches." Filip chose a block of flamed maple that closely resembled the wood he had brought to the machine room. He thought it might have come from the same tree. First he went to the planer and shaved a smooth side, and then the athletic-looking woman reappeared and took up a position on the other side of the band saw. They cautiously guided the wood between them to cut precision slices for guitar sides. The noise was deafening. Filip inspected the first pair and was not entirely satisfied. This illustrated what he had said earlier: that with every cut made while milling or carving, it's possible to find a defect. He cut an extra pair.

He went on, "When I cut for a luthier, I try to be very careful. You go very slowly. If you go fast, you can have bends in the cutting. When

Mihai Filip and assistant cutting guitar sides at Carpathian Tonewood in Râșnov, Romania.

you cut some really good material, you have to be very concentrated, like working with gems. You have to get it right. A little shift, a little pressure put on the wrong side of the wood, can destroy the cut."

I wondered how long one could work carefully and with total concentration in such loud and dangerous circumstances before going crazy or cutting off fingers. Filip outlined the Carpathian Tonewood work schedule. "When I come to work, I expect the employees to do their jobs and make critical decisions. We have workers who do this sort of cut for about one hour, take a break, and put in another hour. Then they shift the kind of work that they do so that they don't have more than two hours on one particular machine. When enough wood piles up, enough merchandise, there will be something else to do. Then you return here again for the precision cutting. We have a man here who cuts two hundred tops or backs in a day. He does this from 8 a.m. to 4 p.m. with an hour break, from noon to 1 p.m. Then he continues 1 p.m. to 4 p.m. with breaks each hour, or even every thirty minutes."

But when I asked about the potential damage to hearing, Filip finally looked concerned. "I wear ear protection, but not all the workers do. They don't understand. I tell them when they are fifty, sixty years old I'll need to yell to get through to them. They're insensitive. I need my ears."

Carpathian Tonewood not only sells to individual luthiers and instrument-making companies but also distributes internationally, to the United States and elsewhere. One customer is John Preston of Old World Tonewood Company, which offers customers Norway spruce and sycamore maple along with red "Adirondack" spruce, which can be found in West Virginia, where the shop is located, and throughout the Appalachian Mountains. As with Norway spruce, the ideal elevation for instrument-quality red spruce is four thousand feet. The wood is often used for guitar tops. The company also sells varnish developed by Eugene Holtier, a Romanian immigrant who became a self-taught luthier after starting out as an industrial design engineer.

Filip and Preston work closely together. "I spoke to John Preston only yesterday. We became good friends, and we've been doing business for about ten, twelve years. He visited here recently, and he came over to the house for a barbecue with my family. We will make barbecue for you too next time."

Filip has yet to travel to West Virginia but already has a good idea of what it looks like. "I think it's beautiful like here. It has wooded mountains like ours. When I talk to John, the weather is exactly the same. When it's sunny out there, it's sunny here. Seventy-five degrees there, seventy-five degrees here. It's the same weather." He paused for a moment, and then said, "But the spruce trees are different, red spruce, no?"

8

Reghin, Romania

THE TOWN OF STRINGED-INSTRUMENT FACTORIES

THE SMALL ROMANIAN CITY of Reghin, located in north-central Transylvania, has been dubbed the "City of Violins." The Calimani and Gurghiu forests have long been sources for excellent resonance wood, and the Mureş river, which runs through the "Italian Valley" (named after the Val di Fiemme), historically provided floatage for numerous logging enterprises in the town. However, in contrast with the instrument-making traditions connected to other European forests, Reghin is a twentieth-century phenomenon.

The city has two major factories producing stringed instruments, several smaller luthier workshops, a large violin store, and two tone-wood milling companies. In the north end of town on Strada Pandurilor stands the Gliga Musical Instrument Factory. Gliga specializes in the violin family of instruments. Vasile Gliga started the factory in 1991 following the fall of the Communist regime, and its products gained a reputation in the United States a decade later when Gliga opened a branch in Pasadena, California. Later, a second branch was established in Vancouver, British Columbia. The company's mission is to provide affordable instruments for anyone in any age group. While a one-sixteenth size violin for a child resembles a toy, Gliga makes the Genial 2-Nitro one-thirty-second size beginner's violin for the "violin girl or boy." In Reghin, Gliga also constructed a compound for workers and visitors with a Gliga restaurant and Gliga market.

Reghin's second factory, Hora SA Musical Instruments, is older than Gliga and considerably larger and more diverse in its products. On my visit to the factory, I was led to the company conference room, which was lined with display racks loaded with violins, guitars, mandolins, ukuleles, bouzoukis, balalaikas, cobzas, panpipes, harps, dulcimers, domras, psalteries, recorders, music stands, and more. The collection also featured children's instruments, including a one-sixteenth size violin for a three-year-old and a muted practice violin to spare households the excruciating struggles of the beginner. Hora has marketed instruments for an array of musical cultures, and the level of instrument quality is based on the musician's level of playing ability. The categories are labeled in descending order: "Academy," "Symphony," "Elite," and "Rhapsody." "Rhapsody" sounds encouraging for beginners ten and under.

The most stunning instrument in the room was an elaborately painted harpsichord, the underside of the lid displaying an example of nineteenth-century naturalism with a ruined castle amid bucolic light and trees, a gorgeous modern version of the instruments that preceded the fortepiano and played for chamber music. The soundboard decorations included blue and yellow Art Nouveau–style chrysanthemums with an intricately carved pattern for the sound hole (called the rose on a harpsichord). The grayish blue with gold trim gave the casing and the legs a stately look. Harpsichord makers almost invariably use Norway spruce for the soundboard, while the casing might be made of linden, poplar, maple, or pine.

A handsome, distinguished-looking man, wearing a red sports jacket over an open-collared gray striped shirt, emerged from the director's office. He introduced himself to me as Nicolae Bazgan, adding that he had worked at Hora as both an engineer and the general manager from its beginning. Knowing that I was an American, he recalled the company's start in distributing to North America. "We started with an instrument company in the New York area, and then we began working with Saint Louis Music, followed by companies in California and Ontario." Hora's ability to distribute to the West, particularly North America, was impressive since it had been a state-owned factory during the Communist period. When I asked about the complications of the time, Bazgan said flatly, "We don't make politics. We make musical instruments. But look, good politics mean a good economy. This is all." Indeed, Hora was making beautiful products for people's pleasure, and at highly affordable prices.

Part of the collection included instruments that were used for research. He moved to a rack of guitars, naming where each came from. "This guitar is from an open street market near here. This Taylor comes from the El Cajon factory near San Diego, and we also have a guitar from the Czech Republic. We started keeping samples because it is very important to know about the level of our competitors and also their prices. We hope to produce better instruments while keeping the price lower."

Turning to the vast array of Hora instruments surrounding the conference room, Bazgan listed the whole gamut of guitars, including "Eurowood" guitars, instruments constructed only of locally accessed wood. They retained the natural look of the wood. He confirmed that local Romanian spruce and maple were used in the making of many Hora instruments, and then continued to the extensive collection of ethnic instruments, picking them up and strumming each briefly so that its individual voice might be appreciated. "We have two workshops. One for violin, viola, cello, and double bass; another for guitars and ethnic instruments. We are always continuing to develop new products. We have friends, musicians, who come in and test instruments to help us improve the quality and playability."

Nicolae Bazgan, general manager of Hora SA Musical Instruments in Reghin, Romania.

Bazgan pointed to some mini-xylophones made as children's toys and picked one up. With a small mallet, he hit the tone bars. "This is my concept. It's simple and logical. The seven sound frequencies correspond to the seven frequencies of light. C, D, E; *do, ré, mi.* Sunlight is divided into frequencies from lower to higher: red, orange, yellow, green, blue, indigo, and violet. Red is the low frequency, then orange, yellow, and so on." He smiled. "It's for kids' workshops."

Bazgan went on to talk of developments in the building of violins, improvements in finishes, and the history of Hora, where he had worked for fifty years. He moved through a collection of photographs hanging on the wall, the first one taken in 1951, when the master luthier Roman Boianciuc and his workshop formed the basis of the Communist-era factory. Bazgan pointed to a picture of himself in 1957. "I started out as a mechanical engineer, and many people ask if I play guitar or violin," he recalled. "I say a little, but if I played better I would want to be a soloist. It's important to increase production and to increase quality, and a soloist could not do this. My being an engineer was not necessary for the company when I started, because the workers then were highly skilled at their craft. Unfortunately, some of our best workers left our factory and opened their own businesses. But as we grew, I improved the machinery and other devices, and production quickly increased. We are now the biggest stringed-instrument-making factory in Europe. We have 270 workers, and each year we produce 50,000 guitars, 5,000 mandolins, more than 3,000 bouzoukis, all based on orders from our customers.

"China is our biggest competitor," he went on. "The Chinese have licenses with Martin, Gibson, Fender, Ibanez, and others for 'remade' guitars. Of course, they're not as good. Violins also can be difficult for them. We have better wood—dried naturally, seasoned ten years, well equilibrated."

Bernard Michaud had been keen to point out the importance of tradition in both forestry and lutherie, and when asked if the Romanians had a long violin-making legacy, Bazgan conceded, "No, we can't say that. The Italians, yes; also the French and the Germans. In those places, if you have a master violin maker, then the father and grandfather had been masters before them. The craft ran in the families. In Romania, in my opinion, this is not the case."

While Bazgan is not a luthier, he studied acoustics and analyzed guitars such as Martins and Taylors. He made structural innovations in the bracing to enhance the passage of sound waves through the instrument's body, thus increasing power. The factory has a laboratory where sound transduction is tested, and Bazgan explained that sound traveled four or five times faster down the grain than across it. He also pulled out another Hora xylophone, this one more like a tiny version of a glockenspiel. A simply crafted wooden box held fourteen metal tubes that, when tapped with a little mallet, rang out brightly with a bell-like sustain. Bazgan played it to demonstrate the mathematical consistency between notes and lengths of the metal tubes.

Like many instrument manufacturers, Hora processes its own wood. "My concept from the beginning has been to have an integrated production, so we buy wood from the west of Romania and the eastern Carpathians. We have a milling facility for preparing wood for tops, sides, and necks, and warehouse quite a large stock. We maintain a ten-year reserve for violins, thirty for cellos, and for guitars, four or five years, because there is a big demand. Oh, and for double bass, three years, no more, because there also is a big market for them."

On the walk to the workshop where instruments of the violin family are made, Bazgan pointed out trees he had planted himself on the factory grounds, representatives of some twenty species. We passed a number of maples in bright yellow leaf next to a group of spruce. The area supervisor opened the door to the workshop, and we beheld a world containing dozens of double basses in all phases of production: some standing in rows, lacquered and awaiting final fixtures; others on cloth-covered tables where two women were at work staining each instrument in turn. Still others were being fitted with black ebony finger boards. Some unfinished instruments were lined up, pale as ghosts, and an enormous supply of necks, tops, backs, and sides lay in neat stacks ready at hand on racks. Some of the double basses were lacquered red, orange, or blue, bright colors like those on the child's xylophone. The violins, violas, violas da gamba, and cellos shared adjacent spaces and spraying and drying rooms. Hora also makes plywood for many of the resistance parts of the instruments, the backs and sides of less expensive instruments.

The robotic machines were fascinating in their own right, above all the computerized carving machine that made spruce tops for the violin family of instruments. A laser traced metal templates for precisely shaping instrument bellies in minutes—a task that takes a luthier days of carving, chiseling, measuring, and finger-plane shaving, all the while adjusting arch and thickness to the qualities of the wood and the front and back pieces. The factory-made instrument lacks the nuances and personality of a handcrafted one, but then most buyers could never afford a luthier's painstaking artistry. The musical instrument business is highly competitive, and at almost every turn a cost-saving machine or protocol has been established. Bazgan had even looked into the possibility of using industrial polyurethane and oil-based varnishes in place of traditional resins as a way of reducing expenses without sacrificing the sound and appeal of a Hora instrument.

Outside the first workshop stood a vast shed that Bazgan commented was used for aging billets. It would be no exaggeration to say that the structure was as long as a football field, the stacked pallets rising easily more than two stories high and at least seventy-five feet across. Billets were separated and spaced with slats between them so that air could circulate readily. Each pallet section was marked with wood identification signs giving the date of cutting, sizes, number of pieces, and the types of instruments they were destined to become. For example, some spruce ribs dated back to July 10, 2000. Another pallet with 850 pieces was designated for soprano ukulele necks. A portion of the shed sheltered a small mountain of sawdust that would eventually be reincarnated as doors, kitchen counter tops, or composite-board siding for new home construction.

The milling area at Hora dwarfed the one at Carpathian Tonewood in Râşnov. Enormous spruce, maple, and beech logs lay on cement supports to prevent them from staining from moisture and molds on the ground. Inside the milling shed, logs were being sent lengthwise down a series of V-shaped rollers for cutting in appropriate lengths before they were quarter-cut and planed. Unlike Filip, Hora factory workers did not pass restless nights over the first split-wood-quality gamble. Some debarking occurred even after the quarter cuts. Still, excellent quality wood was indispensable.

The factory wing contained myriad guitar parts and bodies in various stages of assembly. Long cords wound evenly around the guitars, holding the tops and bottoms in place while the glue dried. One section of the factory contained gorgeous mahogany double f-hole Appalachian dulcimers, with sinuously curved sound boxes. Bouzouki and mandolin bodies awaiting necks resembled empty turtle shells. The balalaikas were perhaps the most striking. Large and triangular, their spruce tops finished to a high gloss, they looked like suspended angels.

The band saws, sanders, and spraying machines, all at work simultaneously, made it difficult to talk; nevertheless, Bazgan exchanged encouraging words with a number of the workers. Toward the end of the wing, along with the stringing room, the factory had a troubleshooting department where work focused on correcting defects in certain instruments to cut down on waste. Finally, packing and shipping areas were strategically located close to the factory entrance.

Near the end of the tour, Bazgan lamented the problems of obtaining good tonewood in Romania. "Our forests are cut without any logic," he complained. "For example, a Turkish-run wood factory here manufactures chipboard, and they cut *everything*. It could be resonance wood or other grade of lumber: doesn't matter. This is poor management of our resources. During the Communist period, there was a regulation that all tonewood would go to Reghin. No one could just cut tone trees. Now anyone can cut wood to make furniture or another product, and they don't respect the large old trees that could be used for musical instruments. Sometimes we bought tonewood from the Turks because I said I could pay more. I would have to beg them to sell me these logs!"

I asked who owned the forests. Are they communal or private? "In the Communist period," Bazgan responded, "the forests belonged only to the state. Now some forests belong to the state, but some lumbering operations steal from them. In private forests, anything can be cut. They don't bother even to save the saplings. They go into chipboard."

He paused, then added glumly, "All of our politicians are gangsters, believe me. Socialist party, liberal party—all. Today they steal from one business, tomorrow from another one. Day after tomorrow, they will steal from me. The president is powerless because all the collaborators are former communists, but not the right communists—third-class, fourth-class communists." It was not the happiest note to end on.

Like Filip, who marked the forests north and east of Reghin, Bazgan mentioned forests in the region Lacul Cuejdel, a lake formed naturally from a large rockfall. The lake attracts photographers because of the mystical effect of reflected light and a remnant forest of tree trunks still standing in the water. The road from Reghin to Lacul Cuejdel passes between Superior Mureş Gorge Nature Park and the Călimani National Park, and just north of the lake is the Vanatori Neamt Natural Park. All of these areas are supposedly protected from clearcutting.

Bazgan's charges of theft and profiteering had merit. The European press supporting environmental protection was particularly angry about forest profiteering in Romania. Greenpeace took up the cause, and environmental groups organized to confront clearcutting operations and lumbering operations on state land in the European Union.

One had only to drive up to nearby forest areas to the east, beyond the Gurghiu river, for example, to find evidence of clearcutting. It looked as if someone had been trying to make very rocky, precipitous pastureland: not a single tree was left standing. Many areas, in fact, appeared just as Bazgan had described, with not a sapling left. Logging activities were overtly in progress, and some trucks were being loaded with very small trees indeed. Nevertheless, the operation may have been entirely legal, with woodcutters being given permission by private owners to denude hillsides.

In a 2015 interview with the Romanian environmental activist Gabriel Paun, head of Agent Green, the BBC journalist Laurence Peter reported that illegal logging had inflicted losses of at least €5 billion (£3.6 billion, $5.7 billion) on Romania since the Communist regime was toppled in 1989. Peter quotes Paun as saying that deforestation had reduced the nation's forest cover to about 26 percent of the total land area, "but scientists say 36 percent should be the minimum." Paun added, "Here the national parks are administered by forestry people, but in other countries the parks administration is independent from forestry."

Laurence Peter also reported that massive Austrian logging operations were under way in Romania. Forced by law to respect their own forests, in which cutting is limited and highly selective, Austrian loggers had turned to corrupt or unregulated neighbors. In May 2018, Romania's Directorate for Investigation of Organized Crime and Terrorism (DIICOT) raided an unprecedented European illegal logging operation connected to Romania's largest timber processor, Holzindustrie Schweighofer. The Austrian company, which supplies do-it-yourself stores and heating pellets, was accused of acquiring timber from illicit suppliers that could not certify the origins of their logs. The US Environmental Investigation Agency estimated in 2015 that up to half of the Romanian logging could be illegal.

The best tonewood comes from old and rare trees, which accordingly have been sacrificed for the making of musical instruments, along with a variety of other exotic woods and animal species from around the world. Identifying where instrument materials originate has become crucial, yet tonewood itself accounts for only a fraction of the massive extraction of lucrative natural materials that has upset global environmental equilibrium. Nevertheless, it provides one more important measure of how forest resources are being exploited.

Some of the most beautiful remaining forest areas lie close to Reghin. To see the "Italian Valley," the Romanian music forests, and Lacul Cuejdel, one must travel northeast along the Mureş river, which flows southwest across Romania and into Hungary. Here it joins the Tisza as a major tributary, coursing south through Hungary and finally forming a confluence with the Danube in Serbia. These rivers cross hundreds of miles and traverse numerous cities, and therefore were vital for transporting goods and floating logs.

The valley runs between the Călimani and Gurghiu ranges; both include national parks. In October the colors of trees reflect on the broad, still parts of the river as it cuts through pastureland and small hayfields. The colorfully painted houses, the animal-drawn vehicles, the dogs running freely or working all give an impression of admirable simplicity and harmony with mountain life. This is also the world of folk music featuring wooden flutes, pipes, and odd, box-shaped violins, along with a three-stringed harmony violin called a *contră,* a specialty of the area. In some parts of Romania, the indigenous gypsy *taraf* is played, sometimes with the three-stringed harmony violin. These instruments and the spirited folk music captured the imagination of Béla Bartók. A synergy exists between instrument making, folk music, dance, and the mountain people.

The valley widens to Gheogheni before heading for Cuejdel Lake in the Stânişoarei Mountains. Here the conifer forests on the limestone uplift mountain formations begin to dominate. Cuejdel Lake is the largest natural dam lake formed in two parts. First a small lake was created by landside on the Cuejdel river in 1978. Then in 1991, following an earthquake the year before and then heavy rains, a much more significant landslide dammed part of the river valley, creating what became a nature park attraction. The spires of half-submerged trees loom above the surface of the water, the reflected sky spreading below them. While Cuejdel Lake is protected, elsewhere submerged wood of various species is coveted by those making furniture, sculpture, and musical instruments.

The town of Bistriţa, famous setting of the Bram Stroker novel *Dracula,* is only forty-five miles north of Reghin. The town is also home to forest manager Silviu Cira. When I met with Bernard Michaud in the Jura to discuss the Risoux forest and told him that I would be visiting Romania, he highly recommended meeting Cira for insight into the Romanian forestry system. Michaud originally met Cira twenty years earlier through connections at the Bois de lutherie and their common interest in forestry, and the two have remained friends since.

Cira sat on a broad couch with a long-haired black-and-white cat in his lap. The cat had an unusual face, split black and white right down the middle. Knowing something of Bazgan's dark vision of local forest management, the evidence of clearcutting practices, and the number of news items revealing illegal logging, I was keen to learn what Cira had to say about the way forests are managed and regulated in Romania. I asked whether the Romanian Department of Forests follows similar forestry management structure and codes to those in Switzerland and France.

"There is a minister who is specifically responsible for the forests and water," Cira said. "It's similar to France—the two resources are regulated together. Romanian forests are managed by a private system and a state one. Until 2000, we had a single system of the state; after that, we created a structure that included private owners. So now the forests, once controlled by the state, have been returned to the original owners, completing the process of restitution. Today more than half of Romanian forests are privately owned."

Mr. Cira confirmed the Greenpeace figure, saying that a little more than a quarter of Romania is forested. "It's not much," he acknowledged, "6.4 million hectares. The greater part of the forested land lies in the Carpathian Mountains and mountain valleys. The national parks are completely protected," he went on. "No one can touch them or the primeval forests, which make up around 300,000 hect-ares altogether—very little. They exist throughout the mountains in parts that are high up and inaccessible." As in Austria, these primeval forests are extant primarily because it is commercially impractical to exploit them.

Mr. Cira was confident that the government maintained strict surveillance over cutting. "Romania has a forest code, laws enacted through the parliament and ministers, and these laws are among the strictest in Europe," he said. "For cutting a small part of the forest, a person must register online a detailed dossier of official papers for the minster so that all activities can be monitored. The government also follows satellite imagery. Each week a team compares images of the forests, and, if they find cutting that does not correspond with the official submitted papers, they alert the departmental minister and the local agency goes out to verify whether the cut is justified or not. It can be determined if the cutting is selective and registered: if not, the penalties for violations can include prison. It is a precise system."

We began to discuss tonewood, and Cira touched on the parts of Romania where good spruce is found, and also the problems created by wind—not just the twisting of tree trunks but also windthrown tree losses. He also lamented the damage done by the bark beetle and strategies for limiting it, including pheromonal manipulation. Bark beetles kill a tree by overcoming its defenses with a mass attack while preparing an environment conducive to their reproduction and the growth of offspring. One strategy for fighting the insect consists of synthesizing the attack pheromone to attract its predators: wood-peckers, wasps, flies, and other beetles.

Cira also offered his own hypothesis on the great mystery of figured maple. If figuring had a genetic cause, he observed, it would be easy to select and cultivate such trees. His own conjecture was that the rare tiger stripe or bird's-eye effect in a trunk was caused by differences in soil composition and the tree's particular disposition to the sun, but he didn't offer further specifics. It is very difficult, even impossible, to be certain which trees contain figuring without cutting into a log or a trunk. Brutally, poachers in Bosnia-Herzegovina and elsewhere, well aware of the value of highly figured wood, are known to simply take crude core samples, leaving stands of damaged trees behind them.

9

Zakopane, Poland, and Luby, Czech Republic

MOUNTAINS AND STRINGED-INSTRUMENT-MAKING SCHOOLS

THE POLISH TOWN OF Zakopane is situated directly south of Krakow on the Slovakian border, where it is surrounded by the High Tatra Mountains, including Gerlachovský štít, the tallest peak in the Carpathians. Rysy, Kasprowy Wierch, Bystrá, and Baníkov peaks also rise near each other in a chain that features high-altitude lakes such as Morskie Oko ("eye of the sea") and hiker-friendly Tichá dolina ("silent valley") and the adjacent Kôprová dolina. On a winter visit, portions of the mountain forests reveal patches of snow where trees are missing. You don't need a satellite to see clearcutting. The practice removes hectares of forest and leaves the remaining trees more vulnerable to damaging storm winds.

Zakopane itself enjoys the distinction of being, for its size, the town situated at the highest altitude in Poland. It's a resort town, known for its skiing, hiking, and thermal baths, as well as for its charming chalets boasting shake roofs and elaborate carvings. Zakopane is the childhood home of master luthier Jan Bobak, who now lives with his family in neighboring Nowy Targ.

Luthier Jan Bobak in Nowy Targ, Poland, near the Tetra Mountains.

Bobak's workshop is located behind the main house, and at its entry hangs an amusing rendition of Marcel Aymé's story "Passe-Miraille" ("walker through walls"). A plaster face sporting a diver's mask appears to emerge from the wall, along with two hands, one clutching a snorkel and the other a crab. Children's toys scattered in the yard provide more evidence of how the Bobak family spirit mixes with their luthier work. When I visited, slabs of flamed maple large enough for a double bass leaned against a turquoise-painted wall. A single billet could also serve as a one-piece back for a cello. These pieces were thick enough to sculpt into instrument backs of whatever depth would be required.

The yard and entry set the tone for the Bobak household, which roiled with domestic chaos, good humor, and hard work. Bobak's younger son, Grzegorz, the new head of Bobak Violino, was at work chiseling the interior of a violin, while Grzegorz's older brother, Maciek—business manager for the family company—discussed the workshop with cheerful enthusiasm when Bobak was momentarily called away for family duties.

Bobak himself looked too youthful for retirement. He was of medium height and dressed casually in a flannel black-, red-, and white-plaid jacket over a black t-shirt. His hair was longish, and he sported a well-groomed silver goatee. His blue eyes gleamed. The workshop consisted of three rooms, one containing a number of violins, a bass, and a piano. A wall was devoted to numerous diplomas and images of Bobak, including stylized artist sketches. He appears in a poster holding a banjo with his group The New Market Jazz Band. On another wall, a horde of family snapshots clustered alongside designs for famous Cremonese violins and cellos. The Bobaks seemed to be well on their way to becoming a generational luthier family, something that Bazgan felt was lacking in Romania. "The violin-making tradition in Poland probably started at the same time as in Italy, the sixteenth century," said Bobak. "We had an Italian queen who came here with Italian musicians and instruments. Stradivari made instruments for the Polish king." Bobak was referring to Sigismund I the Old, who married Bona Sforza of the powerful Milanese family that ruled the Duchy of Milan.

"This was a golden age for Poland," he continued. "So many students from Krakow and other cities would go and study in towns like Padua and Venice in Italy. They also had contact with instruments and violin making, which at that time was fantastic in Italy. In Poland, we had Marcin Groblicz, who made really nice, good-sounding instruments. You can see his violins at the museum in Poznań." Baltazar Dankwart, a contemporary of Groblicz, also figured prominently in the tradition as a court luthier in Warsaw and founder of a family of Polish violin makers.

"In areas like this where there is little industry and not much agriculture, people needed to find some kind of job," Bobak observed. "This is maybe why you see so many instrument makers in the mountains." In a region known for its mountain forests and its highland music, a high school offering instruction and practice in lutherie and wood crafts made eminent sense, and around 1960 one was founded, the Antoni Kenar State Secondary School of Fine Arts.

Bobak's start in lutherie was closely linked to the school. "My father died when I was five years old, killed by a train. My mother was a tailor, and many people, like my uncles, made wooden souvenirs—small animals and other figurines. You can see some of these carvings in Zakopane's shops even today. The administrators decided to set up violin making as a technical high school, and it is fortunate for me that it shared space with the public school. When I was in the sixth or maybe seventh grade, the director of the violin-making school came, and he started to talk to some of us in the public part, trying to interest us in his program. In that instant, I thought, this possibility is really interesting. This is just right for me." Even though he had never worked with wood before, at fourteen Bobak started to learn violin making.

"The school only lasted independently for maybe fifteen years. Then they canceled it. There was no demand for violin makers. I don't know why; it didn't seem logical to me. But they canceled it, and it became a division of the high school. My son Grzeg went there."

"When I started out, I lacked wood, tools, space, everything. It was almost impossible to buy what I really needed from Germany, so I decided to take just any job. I worked for a hospital, then a ski factory. I studied economics, but then I decided at the beginning of the 1980s that I had to make instruments. For many reasons, it was a very difficult period, including the politics of communism. In the meantime, I got married; the house we live in now was my wife's parents' house. Little by little, I started making instruments in the cellar here. Then a Polish violin maker came here from the United States and said that someone in Chicago had created a big workshop and he needed professional luthiers. So I decided to go to Chicago, and though it was complicated getting a passport, I was lucky in the end."

Once settled in Chicago, Bobak began working for William Harris Lee & Co., which was founded in 1978 and still exists, both making and selling violins. The company brought young luthiers from around the world, including graduates of the Cremona Violin Making School and Mirecourt in France. Bobak was part of a group of four luthiers: Japanese, American, French, and Polish. He credits the workshop dynamics and the direction of Tetsuo Matsuda for significantly advancing his career.

"It was a way to make money, but it was also an opportunity to learn. Everyone brought different ideas. This Chicago workshop brought us together, and we shared the experience. I was really happy. I worked there for two years. The expired visa finally said I had to go home. But we cooperated for maybe twenty-five years with the Chicago workshop and sold instruments in the US, Japan, and Europe. Then we decided to go into business by ourselves. As in Chicago, maybe twenty people went through our workshop."

I asked Bobak if different schools or workshops of violin makers have signature sounds. "You know the basic idea, you follow it, but you always have your own ideas," he replied. "Over generations, say in Italy, instrument makers copy great instruments, but then they might think of how to make the rib structure a little different. Or the purfling just a little different, and another generation will repeat it. So it becomes a school."

"But you can also recognize the sounds of individuals. The luthiers always leave their character in the instrument, and yet they are compelled to say each handmade instrument is one of a kind. Each step contains the record of its making, and in this way it is very much like sculpture."

Instruments retain a kind of biography of the person who carved, planed, touched, breathed on, thought over, strategized, and compensated for what could be its faults. Then that biography is absorbed into the story of another person: the musician who plays the instrument. Should it be an excellent stringed instrument that has been well cared for, generations of musicians will add to its voice. Then the discerning listener becomes the end beneficiary.

Forever curious about the role and mysteries of figured maple in lutherie, I wondered if Bobak agreed with some luthiers who argue that flamed maple is stiffer than regular maple or other tonewoods, giving it acoustical advantages for backs and sides. "It's not the flaming that determines the acoustic value," he said. "The figuring is more aesthetic. Probably no one wants to buy a violin that is not flamed. For violas, maybe there is a difference. I have tried many times to make violas with a simple wood, a different wood like poplar or birch, and it sounds beautiful. Why do I try this? Maybe we need to explore a different sound—darker, deeper, while maple gives usually a bright sound, strong but bright. You never see violins with another kind of back and sides. The A string and E string have to be bright, and getting the best quality maple is important."

In light of the dense spruce forests and the altitude around Zakopane and in northern Slovakia, there must have been at one time a wealth of large suitable trees for instrument making. In the early days, Bobak looked for tonewood nearby. "I went into the Tatra Mountains, and east to the part of Poland that is close to Ukraine. The mountains there are not big like the Tatras. You could find really nice maple there in the past, but not anymore—they have a restrictive forest policy now. Trying to find wood was always a kind of adventure—talking to the people, this cutter or another one. Our spruce was very similar to the wood from the Alps, light and flexible. But you need 150-year-old trees. Even if you get an old tree, you cut into it, and the middle might be soft. We have to look for really large trees growing at over three thousand feet. The soil needs to be right, there might be too many branches, and with wind the grain might not be straight inside. It's difficult. We are surrounded by wood, but now we need to look farther away for our materials. Now we get spruce from the Tyrol, and maple from Romania, Ukraine, and Bosnia."

Bobak Violino had grown to include not only Bobak's sons but also several other luthiers in the area. While Grzegorz would follow in his father's footsteps as a luthier, he first studied sculpture at the Kenar School of Fine Arts and then took a master's degree at the Ignacy Jan Paderewski Academy of Music in Poznań. Being in a music academy, students who make instruments also study music. Like Bobak, Grzegorz worked with William Harris Lee & Co. in Chicago and has become a young master luthier in his own right. *Strad* magazine published a profile of Grzegorz revealing a little of his wisdom and humor. "The viola I'm currently working on is based on a Guarneri model and I think it's horribly ugly; the f-holes look like a run-over frog and the scroll appears more like ram's horns. I don't think I've ever seen a truly beautiful viola that also has a perfect sound."

The Bobak Violino workshop began producing over the last few years a new line called Signature Violins. The designs are based on those of four Italian masters: Geovanni Battista Guadagnini, Guarneri del Gesù, Antonio Stradivari, and Carlo Bergonzi. Certain stereotypic characteristics such as projection and brightness distinguish a violin made by the Italian school from French, German, or Polish instruments. I asked if Bobak could identify the different schools. "I can look at an instrument and say, yeah, this is basically French school, or okay, this is German, or this is Polish. There are some common characteristics because people always steal ideas and learn tricks from each other."

Amused, Maciek interrupted: "You stole the knowledge from Chicago." Tetsuo Matsuda had been trained in the Cremona school, and Bobak Violino followed the Italian school via the unlikely route of the United States. Maciek did not inherit his father's or brother's passion for carving and assembling instruments and instead pursued studies in business, later taking jobs in marketing. As Bobak Violino grew, Maciek served the family firm well as its business manager. The Bobak Violino display was by far the most dramatic at the Cremona Mondomusica and other international expositions. The delicately crafted violins stood in contrast with sepia photo enlargements of a fire-ravaged concert hall with charred walls and columns. Another row of gorgeous instruments stood in front of a half-burnt piano. I asked where the images came from, and Maciek said, "I found them on the internet and thought the colors and the contrasting images would be powerful visually." One paradoxical display featured an enlarged sepia photograph of the cold gears of machinery with the words "brilliant," "open," "warm," "resonant," "singing," and "sweet" superimposed in yellow lettering. This panel served as a backdrop for a row of Bobak violins and violas on sale.

When Bobak was called away, Maciek talked for a while about Polish highlander music. "The Zakopane folk music has become a very popular attraction. They never use trumpets or clarinets as in other parts of Poland—just bowed instruments, two violins. One violin plays solo, another plays chords. There are variations with singers and dancing at festivals, but they commonly play in the restaurants and bars." The groups also play two local stringed instruments, one an *ocalone gęśle* and the other a lower-pitched *złóbcoki,* both of which look like elongated ancestors of the modern violin. These are known as "carved violins" because the backs, sides, and neck of both are fashioned out of a single piece of maple. As with a violin, Norway spruce is used for the tops.

Bobak's hometown of Nowy Targ has served as the traditional capital of the Podhale region, also known as the Polish highlands. Highlander music is closely associated with the Gorals, an ethnic group whose members have historically thrived as shepherds on both the Polish and the Slovakian sides of the Tatra Mountains. Goral music, dance, and traditional dress add to the cultural texture of the region and reinforce the sense of resourcefulness and creativity of mountain people. Some of the traditional music has evolved into popular Polish music and is performed internationally, as with the Trebunie-Tutki Family folk group.

Bobak had made a key point about living in the mountains, the lack of jobs, and the ingenuity that can go into crafts. Perhaps one of the best examples of this may be seen in the western Czech Republic town of Luby on the German border. As in Zakopane, a formal lutherie school was established there, but Luby's was nearly a century older. The town was formerly called Schönbach until the Germans were forced out after World War II, when officials gave it a Czech name. In fact, Schönbach had once been known as the "Austrian Cremona" based on the reputation of its instrument makers.

In the sixteenth century, cinnabar mining brought a population of workers and musicians to the Luby area. Cinnabar is a bright red mercury sulfide ore that has been used for coloring since Roman times, and is also the source of the refined mercury element. Miners and their families in the region supplemented their incomes through participation in making violin-family instruments—or at least parts for them. A Czech entrepreneur named Richard Dotzauer worked to develop economic opportunities in the Ore Mountains just south of Luby and the Giant Mountains on the border with Poland. Along with initiatives for establishing schools for embroidery, he took it upon himself in 1873 to create one of Europe's most important violin schools.

The complicated history of the Luby violin school mirrors the political and social upheavals that have periodically gripped the area since the 1870s. The school began by offering musical training in the form of home instruction, but very soon more formal training was being offered at the Schönbach town hall. The curriculum included the making of guitars and violin family instruments, as well as the preparation of sheet music for publication. Construction began in 1912 for the music school building—a three-story, stolid block architecture with wood paneling and a central staircase. When the Cremona factory was established in 1922, Luby was on its way to becoming an instrument-making center. The industry quickly expanded and in 1927 commemorated its workers with the Violin Maker Monument, a tribute to all the unknown instrument crafters in Luby. The monument consists of a globe set on a pedestal comprising four violin scrolls carved out of limestone. A bronze-cast, aproned luthier stands on top of the world looking into the f-hole treble area on the belly of a violin.

In 1938, Germany annexed the western Czechoslovakian border areas and, a year later, seized the entire country, a prelude to the invasion of Poland. The upheaval of World War II disrupted instrument making in the region. After the war, the local German population, including over a thousand instrument makers, was expelled. Germany already had two instrument-making centers in Mittenwald and Markneukirchen. A group of the expelled Schönbach luthiers, who maintained the spirit and tradition of the Czech school, created a third center in Bubenreuth near Nuremberg. The new Czech administration changed the name Schönbach to Luby, and the school became a Communist program and then continued as the Cremona cooperative until the Velvet Revolution in 1989. Strunal Schönbach Musical Instruments took over, growing into a mass-production factory making 150,000 instruments a year, with a large market in North America.

In 2005 the violin-making school moved to Cheb, located only twenty miles from Luby. The school's building in Cheb is a converted apartment building bearing a black stone plaque with gold lettering commemorating the town's synagogue, which had been burned on Kristallnacht, and the demise of the local Jewish population. The apartment building now accommodates carving benches, racks of tools, varnishes, and tonewood for the violin instruments and guitars. The school is part of the larger Integrated Secondary School of Cheb and is one of only a handful of active instrument-making technical schools left in Europe.

I had stopped by Strunal Schönbach Musical Instruments to see its museum, which turned out not to be open, but the receptionist phoned Ondřej Kubart, the Strunal Instruments director of sales, who generously offered to give me a factory tour. Kubart was somewhere in his thirties, had short, dark blond hair with longish sideburns, and wore stylish rectangular glasses. His manner was robust and good-humored, a different sort of guide from Bazgan, manager of Hora. Kubart had previously worked for Nestlé and Strunal had hired him, appreciative of his affability and his gift for languages.

Unlike Reghin, where the Hora factory was established in 1961 and Gliga Musical Instruments even more recently, Strunal started with the demise of the Habsburg empire in 1918 and endured the Great Depression, the Nazi occupation, and Communist state ownership, only to become a capitalist company again, struggling with the elemental issues of competition, modernization, and competitive wages.

Kubart showed me through the Strunal display room, where black-and-white photographs dating back decades showed massive spruce trunks being transported to Luby. "For instruments using solid wood, we need really good quality materials, and it can take twenty years to process it," Kubart commented. "The wood we buy is stocked for fifteen years to dry, with no humidity at all. Then after fifteen years we move it to a stockroom maintained at sixty degrees. This is where the wood is prepared for production."

Kubart held up one of the Strunal classical guitars. "We sell this in every country. It's our best-selling guitar, 4855. We identify our instruments by number rather than by name." The 4855 is a low-priced, respectable student guitar with a cedar top and laminated mahogany back and sides, mahogany neck, and tempered beech fret board. It is available in sizes ranging from one-eighth to full-sized. While the

Strunal guitar tops are generally made of solid spruce or red cedar with wooden rosettes outlining the sound hole, the backs and sides may be walnut, Santos rosewood, Indian rosewood, red gum, and tineo, as well as mahogany. Often, however, they are laminated rather than solid wood.

Gesturing toward an array of stringed instruments, Kubart continued, "We have some excellent instruments here from the masters in Luby, like Schneider and Zakopcanik. They made instruments with an original sound. However, the instruments we manufacture today are mostly for children and beginners. Our most expensive guitar costs approximately $600 while a guitar made by an outside master probably starts at about $2,500."

Upstairs, Kubart opened the door to an entirely different class of instruments. "These are all made by Strunal too. They are old, and we don't produce such instruments anymore. This cello, for example, is worth about $120,000. These others, too, are the work of old masters." Cards identified the maker of each instrument, along with the place and date of manufacture, which in a few cases was as early as the 1920s. "All of these instruments were made in the home or in a small room, and not in the factory. We keep some historic instruments, not only ours but also some from India and other Asian countries."

"This," he said, selecting one elegant specimen, "is our masterpiece double bass. It won a prize in international competition and has very good sound, so we take it to more competitions and exhibitions and say that although this one is not for sale, we can make basically the same instrument for a customer who wants it." The company's custom-built instruments make an impressive and lucrative sideline that favorably compares with other manufacturers' mass-produced instruments.

Strunal has also sold instruments boasting particular innovations. One was a misfit double bass better described as having an "abbreviated body." Kubart explained, "This is the invention of the master David Gage from New York. He was building the double basses, and he thought all his life how to make a travel double bass, one that was not so big, not so heavy, but still maintained the same strong sound. Strunal can also put a pickup in it and make it electric, and the adjustable bridge is our invention." He pulled the scroll off the top of the neck and laughed. "We joke to customers it's broken." David Gage thought of every way to abbreviate his bass. He named his invention the "Czech-Ease Road Bass." Strunal acquired the rights to manufacture and distribute it in Europe, and Gage's company distributes it in the Americas.

While we were looking at violins, Kubart showed me a new Strunal product. "This cello comes from a set of quartet instruments. We don't have all the instruments here because Jaroslav Svěcený, one of our most famous violin players, has the viola and two violins at home. He plays them but normally they stay together like a quartet. So these instruments can't be sold alone." I was reminded of Paganini's Stradivarius quartet, and Bobak Violino had showed me their quartet package. Does a set of quartet instruments created by the same maker provide a more harmonious voice? The concept was intriguing.

We looked at some master guitars, each with a certifying label below the sound hole. Kubart turned our conversation to the difficulties of selling guitars, which revealed other poignant struggles that Strunal was suffering. "We don't sell many guitars. The buildings may need to be rebuilt because the costs of electricity, heating, and water are too high, and we start to see these costs in the price of the instruments. Our dealers and distributors say, 'We don't want your guitars. They are too expensive for us. We can have the same guitar cheaper from Spain.' The competition in the guitar market is our biggest difficulty. We need to do something about it, but we don't have 100 million crowns to build a completely new company. With violins, violas, cellos, and basses, it's no problem."

I commented that Hora logically would represent a major source of competition. "Yes, because they are new," Kubart responded. "This is an old capitalist factory. Every machine is old. Two or three years ago when it looked like the company would fold, a financial group from Prague bought it. They put some money in and started a new production style, but it takes two years to see how profitable it will be. We have big orders from the USA and from Russia for thousands of cellos and violins, but we cannot produce them. In the old times, there were six hundred people at the factory, and now there are ninety."

The problem of housing and providing for six hundred workers seemed daunting. Luby is not a large town. "They lived here," Kubart explained to me. "There was the school, and the students would come every second week and work for the company. After they finished their studies, they would work for Strunal for three years, and then they'd go. Now the school is in Cheb, and the building where the students lived is closed. This area collapsed economically in two years, and now only the company is left. The workers go to Germany because they receive better pay. They have families, and they can't live with our wages." Clearly, Hora enjoyed a much more favorable economic environment from a hiring standpoint.

Programmed violin-carving machine, Strunal Schönbach Musical Instruments factory in Luby, Czech Republic.

Master luthier at Strunal Schönbach Musical Instruments factory in Luby, Czech Republic.

The basic facilities for making musical instruments at Strunal resembled those at Hora: enormous storage buildings, areas for aging wood, a milling area, and a plywood-making press, large noisy cutting and carving spaces, quieter assembly areas, and varnishing and finishing rooms. But large parts of the factory lay dormant, including the central heating plant that was once fired with tree trunks and waste wood. Now the factory uses gas. Still, despite the mournful impression it gave and the tectonic changes that were taking place in this historic musical-instrument-making region, the old factory retained an appealing aura, in part because its friendly older workers focused on producing extremely well-made instruments for a relatively modest price.

Strunal also made strings, but Kubart explained that this part of the company was being phased out by the end of the year because of European Union laws regarding the nickel component, rightly deemed dangerous for the environment and a hazard for workers. The company could not afford to make the necessary economic accommodation for using toxic metals. The rows of unused machines accentuated the point: only two women were occupied with spinning fine metal wire over silk threads.

The history of the factory was poignant, and I wished keenly that it should flourish. Kubart passed through a violin-finishing area and climbed the stairs to a space that felt oddly private, even though it was at the very heart of the factory. "In this space," Kubart announced, "are the masterpiece violins." One lean, handsome luthier, maybe forty, worked alone in front of a cluttered desk arranged to suit his personal manner of working. He was flanked by rows of violins and violas and was busy rubbing stain into one. He looked up and smiled warmly at us as if he were a living artifact of the former craft world of Luby. Kubart introduced him as "our standard, our master."

10

Mirecourt, France, and Andelusia, Spain

THE GUITAR-MAKING TRADITION

LIKE MANY MUSICAL INSTRUMENTS with appealingly curved forms, frequently played in intimate settings, the guitar and its predecessors appear in European paintings from the Renaissance to modern times. The Spanish vihuela appeared in Bernadino Pinturicchio's 1493 fresco *Music,* in the Vatican and later in Juan de Juanes sixteenth-century painting of an angel musician. Vermeer's 1672 painting *The Guitar Player* depicts an instrument that would steadily evolve in form and popularity. Picasso's *The Old Guitarist* has become a reproduction favorite.

Initially, guitars were appreciated in Renaissance Italy and France. The Violin Museum in Cremona displays the Antonio Stradivari Sabionari 1679 guitar. Its lovely pure tones can be heard on museum recordings. Guitar masters used the instrument to play works by Santiago de Murcia Angelo and Michele Bartolotti. Stradivari, Amati, and Guarneri made a number of guitars, and five Stradivarius guitars exist, though at present the Sabionari is the only one that is playable, having been restored in the early 1800s and again in 2011. In 1948 Andrés Segovia left his signature and dedication to Stradivari in the Sabionari under the sound hole, neither the first nor the last musician to leave some mark on a revered instrument. Louis XIV's favorite instrument was the guitar, and the ones he played look very much like the Stradivarius and others of the period. These guitars have double strings, four or five pairs, like most mandolins of today, and an elongated body with a subtler waist than contemporary guitars. Some have elaborately carved geometric patterned rosettes set within their sound holes, as one sees in Vermeer's *The Guitar Player*.

The story of the guitar seems to be as unclear as the violin's. Did it originate in India or was it a North African instrument that made its way through Spain? Was it developed over centuries as an offspring of the *cithara*, the instrument Nero supposedly played in the official music and poetry competitions he established? *Cithara* is the root for the names of several important popular instruments, most notably the guitar. "Guitar" is derived from the Spanish *guitarra*, which in turn comes from the Old French *guiterre* or *guiterne*, which is based on the Latin *cithara* and the Greek *kithara*. Even the *sitar—si*, three, plus *tar*, strings—from Old Persian is part of the mix. It's easy to see the zither or cither as a cithara relative.

The guitar as we know it today is considered the second most popular instrument in the world, closely following the piano. On the one hand, it provides limitless musical possibilities for virtuoso players; on the other, any person with a modicum of ability can within a very short time learn simple chord progressions, create rhythm, and accompany singing. Guitars are substantially more player-friendly than the (unfretted) quartet instruments, on which the notes must be found, and for which bowing technique is critical. Many amateur guitar players are self-taught and enjoy creating variations of popular songs or even composing songs of their own.

In the United States, inexpensive Harmony Silvertone Guitars, electric and acoustic, were sold from Sears, Roebuck, and Company catalogues, and some believe this availability helped change American music. For example, in the early twentieth century, Mississippi

Delta blues artists, whose music was rooted in rural poverty and hard agricultural work, would often make their own instruments. The single-stringed diddley bow, the forerunner of the slide guitar, was developed by attaching baling wire to a barn wall and stretching it over a thread spool or a snuff can serving as a bridge. Nails, knives, and bottles served as sliders on the strings, creating one of the key musical features of the blues and later jazz, note bending and rhythmic techniques for emotional expression. Free diddley bows, played on the lap or held like a guitar, might use a broomstick with a stretched wire and a cigar box resonator. The musician achieves singing tones, sustain, and vibrato characteristic of Delta blues. Soon, through Sears and the emerging instrument factories such as Oscar Schmidt Company, maker of the Stella, musicians could acquire affordable portable instruments, primarily guitars and harmonicas. These budget instruments provided rhythmic and harmonic support for vocal expressions—thoughtful, mournful, or fiery. Guitars began to find an American identity featured in cowboy music, country and western, bluegrass, folk, blues, jazz, and rock and roll. Even an old Harmony Silvertone advertisement headline, "The Resonance of Wood," invoked impressive American materials by depicting a guitar at the base of a massive California redwood.

At international guitar expositions these days, guitars made from cigar boxes and steel cans or featuring resonators are often seen. These improvised instruments seem to be enjoying a nostalgic revival. Even in Paris, cigar box guitars, already assembled or in kits containing accessories such as pickups and glass bottle necks, can be purchased from a company called Blues Guitars France. Ironically, they are quite expensive.

Jan Bobak referred to the economic resourcefulness of the mountain people, but ingenuity is also reflected in their music and dance, adapted and evolving from an array of local and traditional influences. These poor regions inspired a mix of homemade instruments. A cigar box fiddle might be cobbled together and accompanied by a washboard (played rhythmically with thimbles) and a washtub bass to keep the beat. One can follow music trails down through the Blue Ridge Mountains to mountain music heritage museums and musical festivals, or turn west into Tennessee.

Resourcefulness and innovation in music making were far from limited to mountain people. In late nineteenth-century New Orleans, groups of young people trying to earn some pocket change by performing on the streets formed "spasm bands" in which they played cigar box instruments, spoons, gourds, metal pipes, and almost anything that could lend tone and rhythm. Some of this music contributed to the development of Dixieland and the roots of jazz. Jug bands, important in the evolution of the blues, performed in Memphis and Nashville, iconic cities for music performance and recording. A jug player blew tones over the lip of a jug and other makeshift instruments, including stovepipes played in a similar manner and comb-and-paper kazoos. American jug bands influenced the later music genre called skiffle, a form of folk music with jazz or blues inflections that became highly popular in the United Kingdom in the 1950s with the songs and performances of the popular guitarist and singer Lonnie Donegan and others. Skiffle, with some of its social themes, led in part to the later emergence of British rock, including punk rock. Stringed instruments are a common part of these varieties of music, the guitar being among the most prominent. Skiffle, in particular, brought the guitar into prominence in popular British music. In extraordinary ways, British bands such as the Rolling Stones would invigorate Americans' interest in their own musical inventions and in Black musical artists in particular. The name Rolling Stones is itself derived from a Muddy Waters song, "Rollin' Stone."

While the guitar has at least a five-hundred-year history, with ancestors of even greater vintage, its popularity increased dramatically in the twentieth century. Already a versatile instrument on which a musician could play chords, melody lines, and even percussion, innovations gave the guitar a bigger, more varied voice. Traditional versions of the guitar were improved for different genres of music. At the same time, popular music was evolving and expanding, and with the arrival of amplification, radio, and then television, the instrument appeared literally everywhere—at dances, in concert halls, and as part of variety shows. Many American adolescents have attempted to play one.

The flat-topped and arch-topped guitars used in American music evolved directly from the guitar developed in the Classical and Romantic periods. The famous Neopolitan luthier Ferdinando Gagliano in 1774 may have been the first to introduce a guitar with five single, rather than paired, strings. Gagliano's Neapolitan guitar heralded significant changes that provided musicians with more tonal and ornament options. Gagliano and later innovators saw a precedent in stringing changes that evolved for the lute between 1590 and 1650. Traditionally lyres had six courses of paired gut strings and the single, highest string, called a chanterelle. Luthiers changed the adjacent course to the second highest string, called the sottana. These single strings offered musicians clearer, more individuated notes, and at the same time facilitated ornaments such as trills, hammer-ons, vibrato, and slurs, some performed with the left hand and others plucked with the right cross string. Gagliano transformed the baroque guitar from five courses of double strings to five single strings, allowing the musician to execute more stylistic versatility. The shift to single strings was a critical step in the evolution of the classical guitar as we know it today. The addition of a sixth single string became the crowning development. The origin of the sixth string is not clear, but it may have been an Italian innovation, if one is to judge by a 1779 Gaetano Vinaccia guitar, the oldest extant specimen.

Romantic era guitar luthiers used only spruce for the tops, but more variation occurred in the wood types employed for the back and sides. While figured maple was most common, many other woods were used, including imported mahogany and Brazilian rosewood. Primarily used in fine furniture making, rosewood and mahogany also provided outstanding tone in stringed instruments.

Mirecourt, France, and Andelusia, Spain

Schools of guitar making gradually emerged, with master luthiers gaining inspiration from musicians and composers alike. Gennaro Fabricatore, also from Naples, began making guitars at the end of the eighteenth century and continued until close to the time of his death in 1832. Mario Guiliani, who owned a Fabricatore six-stringed guitar and was an early nineteenth-century virtuoso who wrote guitar concertos, transformed the status of the guitar among stringed instruments. Johann Georg Stauffer in Vienna added such innovations as a curved back, narrow waist, and extended fingerboards to guitars during the first half of the nineteenth century. Schubert played a Stauffer and produced compositions that included guitars. Stauffer's in-line tuning key arrangement would one day be copied by both the C. F. Martin and Fender companies.

France has been one of the greatest contributors to classical guitar making over the centuries and continues to be. One of the most recognized guitar luthiers of the Romantic era was Pierre-René Lacôte, an apprentice to the Parisian luthier Joseph Pons, whom Empress Marie-Louise had commissioned to make a guitar for virtuoso Mauro Giuliani. Pons's notable innovations included Y-shaped soundboard bracing, neck/heel and head joints, locking ling nut friction pegs, and one-piece backs. Lacôte refined and modified these contributions and introduced his own improvements, such as a slant soundboard bracing and lowered action.

Etienne Laprévotte, a French master guitar luthier and a contemporary of Lacôte, was born in Mirecourt, although he too would ultimately live and work in Paris. He invented guitars with round, maple-domed backs and round necks.

During the nineteenth century, numerous guitar luthiers set up workshops in France, primarily in Mirecourt and Paris. French guitars became noted for their characteristic sound and personality, excelling in bright trebles, appealing tone, and fullness of voice. The French guitars of the Romantic period gained an identity associated with Mirecourt, home to one of the most rigorous of the state-supported

European instrument-making schools, in addition to a four-century history at the heart of France's lutherie legacy. Mirecourt enjoys a propitious location for lutherie—near the Vosges, a low mountain region that supplied tonewood maple, and with ready access to spruce from the Jura and the Prealps. The National School of Lutherie at Mirecourt maintains an exceptional reputation, admitting only twenty students at a time out of approximately two hundred applicants.

To this day, Mirecourt is full of active lutherie workshops in the community, and the best students from the school often intern with them, making instruments that are not necessarily those directly connected to the curriculum. These instruments include guitars, ukuleles, and mandolins, among others. One luthier workshop closely associated with the Mirecourt tradition is l'Atelier Gérôme Frères, established in 1892. Louis Gérôme arrived from Paris at the end of the nineteenth century and began making mandolins in Mirecourt, eventually turning to guitars, with family luthier successors. More recently, a former Mirecourt student, Philippe Monneret, apprenticed with Gérôme Frères, and the older generation eventually ceded the atelier to him. In an interview on French television, Monneret discussed the interdependence of skilled woodworking and sonority in the tradition of Gérôme Frères and Mirecourt in general. Every step in construction affects the sound of an instrument, and thus every artisan-made instrument is different. "It takes a very long time to understand this relationship," he observed. "I started on the string quartet instruments, and when I shifted to making mandolins and guitars, it took me ten years to understand how these instruments function." Monneret emphasized the fact that factory-made instruments could never achieve the optimal sonority of those crafted by hand because a luthier had the ability to address both the distinctive qualities of the wood and the tensions of the structure.

The Musée de la lutherie et de l'archèterie françaises in Mirecourt displays a broad diversity of stringed instruments, along with diagrams explaining the steps involved in making a violin, cello, or a bow. The display focuses on a kind of freak show of inventiveness: conjoined violin and viola, weird snaky bows, guitar-violins, and an eight-string guitar-lyre. The museum itself seems to wrap around an enormous double bass. While this centerpiece, which stands nearly two stories tall, was built for emblematic effect, the octobass, nearly twelve feet tall and weighing nearly three hundred pounds, is a rare specialty of Mirecourt luthier Jean-Jacques Pagès. To play it, a musician must stand on a platform and employ a system of levers and pedals, in addition to a bow. Having received an order for two of the instruments from the Montreal Symphony Orchestra, Pagès modernized the work of its inventor, Jean-Baptiste Vuillaume, so that his own specimens would be mechanically reliable and have greater musical range.

Given that Mirecourt in the past featured portraits of its master luthiers, all male, and provided a synopsis of their contributions, the museum recently undertook an initiative to recognize women luthiers and composers. The museum's tribute fits especially well now that the elite instrument-making school has finally achieved parity in the admission of young women and men.

The violin-making tradition gradually arrived at, and has adhered to, a strict formula for the materials, but guitar luthiers continue to experiment; today they also take environmental sustainability into consideration when selecting tonewoods. However, the more rigid traditional requirements imposed by violinists on luthiers have now come to apply to flamenco guitars. Invariably these have spruce tops and cypress backs and sides, along with specific design features that differ from those of other guitars. For top-quality classical guitars, traditional expectations apply too, primarily with regard to the use of spruce and Brazilian rosewood.

Many top guitar luthiers are unshakable in their opinion that Brazilian rosewood offers optimal tonal qualities, and speak wistfully of its rich dark red coloration, its attractive grain pattern, and even its rose perfume. Nevertheless, they are now forced to find alternatives.

Brazilian rosewood is high on the list of endangered species after tropical tree exploitation went unchecked for two centuries. Brazilian rosewood has been imported for over three hundred years and was used as a tonewood even for Renaissance instruments. It developed into a nearly indispensable back and side tonewood component of classical guitars. Importation of Brazilian rosewood is carefully regulated, and any products using it, such as furniture or guitars, must be registered. CITES, the Convention on International Trade in Endangered Species, established legislation protecting both wildlife and forests. The regulations apply internationally in an attempt to stem the rampant overcutting and exploitation that have taken place over the centuries.

Brazilian rosewood trees, *Dalbergia nigra,* grow to height of up to 125 feet and a diameter of three to four feet—a suitable size for guitar backs. The coloration and grain patterns vary considerably and can be spectacular. The cross cut of a trunk will show heartwood interiors with astonishingly deep colors, chocolate or dark plum. Spanish and Portuguese explorers, on discovering the unusually rich colors and attractive grain patterns, brought the wood back with them to Europe. Brazilian rosewood rapidly became a prized material for cabinets, furniture, and paneling, as well as for musical instruments.

The Mirecourt registry of guitars in its collection shows the materials that were used in the eighteenth and nineteenth centuries. The older guitars used spruce, maple, and ebony, as did the quartet instruments, but also included ivory or bone frets and mother of pearl decorations. Rosewood appears in early nineteenth-century guitars, as does mahogany. With strict environmental controls now in place, lists of tonewood substitutions for back and sides are continually being proposed.

Spanish luthiers have established their own guitar-making legacy based on musical traditions that included guitar-like instruments. For centuries, Spain and North Africa provided a conduit for instruments to Western Europe from the Near and Far East. Instruments—precursors of the violin and the guitar—and ethnic folk music forms came through this route. One of the most significant confluences of Eastern and Western cultures occurred in Andalusia—Cordoba, Granada, and Seville—the heart of Spanish guitar making.

The spirit of music is so ingrained in Andalusia that one is hardly surprised that Spanish folk, flamenco, or classical music can be heard throughout the cities. Neighborhood groups may use the smallest cafés as practice spaces, or five everyday people might show up in an empty bar late in the evening and take turns singing flamenco—improvising, challenging each other. In gospel, blues, and jazz, singers and musicians feed off each other, and flamenco is no different. The songs are sharp, rhythmic, and fiery, a musical battle of emotional life or death. The passion of the music can be felt intimately even in large public performances.

In local informal contexts, musicians may play guitars, but also the bandurria, a squat, twelve-stringed instrument sometimes mistaken for a mandolin. Versions of the bandurria date back to the sixteenth century, and from Spain it made its way to the New World Spanish colonies in Central and South America and the Philippines. The instrument blends wonderfully with voice and guitars. Likewise, the Spanish vihuela, which looks like a synthesis of lute and guitar, became an important instrument in Italy and Portugal as early as the fifteenth century. Mexican mariachi groups play modern, much-revised versions of this early Renaissance instrument. Ultimately, the nineteenth-century Spanish masters Antonio de Torres and José Ramírez III transformed classical guitar design into the instrument known today.

Although Spain is ringed with mountains and the Atlas range runs through neighboring Morocco, classical guitar tonewood is not indigenous. The region is too arid to support Norway spruce, so luthiers have historically relied on imported tonewood from Central Europe. Spanish cypress was once readily available and is the essential tonewood for the body of a flamenco guitar. Nevertheless, flamenco guitar tops require spruce, which comes to Spain from the Alps.

In Granada, highly respected luthiers have their guitar workshops in the old Jewish quarter called Realejo, just below the Alhambra. One of the most famous is Guitarrería Casa Ferrer. The workshop was founded by Benito Ferrer Martín in 1875. Now in its fourth generation of guitar luthiers, the Ferrer family is proud of their relationship with the Japanese company Yamaha. Eduardo Ferrer served for several years as a design consultant for some of Yamaha's classical guitar models while also working with Japanese apprentices.

Just six blocks from Casa Ferrer is the Daniel Gil de Avalle guitar shop. Gil de Avalle was born in 1961 and grew up at the end of the Francoist era in an accomplished musical family. He studied piano at Centro Artistico y Literario and violin at the Conservatory of Granada, followed by a stint at the Conservatory of Madrid, where he claims that the odors of woodwork seduced him into his craft. His list of regional and national awards shows him to be a remarkable artisan, the Spanish equivalent of a Japanese living cultural treasure.

In contrast with the Ferrer store, which is small and focuses exclusively on family-made guitars, the Gil de Avalle shop has showcases containing racks of violins, violas, guitars, and bandurrias. The company also sells cello cases, music stands, and old instruments. An old fretted concert zither, a Spanish laud (a stringed instrument in the cittern family), mandolins, and antique guitars are hung together on one wall of the store. Most of the guitars on sale are locally made or come from Asia, but Gil de Avalle's own handcrafted guitars are featured exclusively in a showcase near the luthier workshop. Gil de Avalle keeps a private collection of historic guitars, which he uses as models for carefully rendered reproductions. The originals include works by some of the greatest names and families of luthiers in Spanish guitar-making history, including José Pernas, José Ortega, and Joséf Pagés.

Granada, with its long guitar-making tradition, continues to attract luthiers, and their shops are prevalent in Realejo. "There are about thirty guitar luthiers established in Granada, and more young people are setting up their workshops all the time," Gil de Avalle remarked. "Guitar making here dates back to the nineteenth century, and it remains because of a tradition of the artisans, ebonists, and instrument makers. There are documents that prove guitars existed here in the fifteenth century. We have a professional guitar-making school, and young people acquire guitar-making skills mainly through apprenticeships. It's a bit like Mirecourt and Cremona, but for guitars."

I asked him how he became a luthier, and he exclaimed, "The smell of wood! I liked the aroma. When I was growing up, there were many furniture makers here as well as luthiers, and I could always smell the wood. In the old days, I even cut the trees with my mentor and varnished instruments, of course. But now many luthiers don't have the time for that and send their guitars away for varnishing rather than doing it themselves. There are specialists for varnish. A guitar may be less delicate than a violin, but still the varnish needs to be clean and even."

In factories, varnish or polyurethane is applied with spraying machines in ventilated rooms and cubicles. A luthier's workshop is orderly and well vacuumed, in part because dust is a constant concern when varnishing (although some dust can be removed with light sanding before applying additional coats). Gil de Avalle has a preference for the traditional French polish, a high-gloss technique with layers of shellac thinned with denatured alcohol. The new varnishes and lacquers offer much more protection, but the effect on tonality and volume is not the same.

Gil de Avalle continued, "I started by restoring quartet instruments. I learned about the chemistry of varnishes and how to apply them. I experimented with making bowed instruments. Then I worked with a master guitar maker in Granada for fifteen years and acquired the essential knowledge. Everyone wants to be a luthier in the first month, but it takes at least ten years to learn to make a really good guitar, never earlier than that. During the first ten years, the group shows you how to work, and after you can learn what you want."

When I asked Gil de Avalle how he would characterize the particular voice of his own instruments, he responded, "We all look for differences having to do with organological characteristics. If I make an imitation of a Torres guitar, it sounds like Torres." Gil de Avalle was referring to the legendary nineteenth-century Spanish luthier Antonio de Torres, who is credited with establishing the structural and tonal fundamentals for the modern classical guitar. Some like to compare his guitar design contributions to those Stradivari made for the violin.

"You always have to think at a different level. If you choose a certain thickness, a certain voice, it comes from your sensitivity, and the guitar behaves differently according to the tensions. Physically, the tensions are a very important part of the guitar. It's like a picture: one part is the lines, but another is the message. Some guitars inspire you and others don't. It's not furniture. Making a chair is easy, but making a chair that can speak is difficult."

Making a guitar speak is just part of the process of developing a signature sound in a stringed instrument. "Of course, each guitar is a little different, depending on your philosophy, your approach to the materials, how you perceive the sound, its dynamics, its equilibrium, its soul."

As mentioned previously, Hermann Hauser developed refinements to guitar making that would produce the sound that Segovia yearned for, one with soul. The Hauser surpassed, in Segovia's estimation, the Ramirez guitar that he performed and recorded with for so long. Professional guitarists typically seek an instrument with both playability and a voice that inspires them. Sometimes a musician will discover an instrument that is a revelation, leading to a new musical direction, to nuances in style. This can occur in a recording studio, the producer pushing a musician for a qualitatively different sound. Some studios keep a collection of guitars, and the engineers may suggest one to inspire creative change. Or a musician may ask a luthier to alter an instrument in ways the player believes will produce the desired sound.

"Guitarists request the changes they want. In the seventies, the shape was different; the guitar had a shorter neck. Then it was changed for the musician's comfort, and the luthier makes the adjustments work. Even different weather conditions can affect the sound. For example, Barcelona is very dry, which makes the wood light. You learn from working in different places."

Atlantic winds arrive in Barcelona with low humidity, which contributes to the dryness of the area. Wood seasoned for thirty years in Barcelona will have a considerably different character from wood seasoned for the same period in the Jura or in Northern Italy. However, Gil de Avalle dismissed the idea of different cities having different guitar-making identities. "Luthiers are very individualistic," he affirmed.

Anyone who travels through Spain these days, and especially through Andalusia, might believe that the countryside has become one enormous olive grove. Spain is the world's biggest producer of olive oil. About 2.4 million hectares of land are dedicated to its production—twice as many as in Italy and three times as many as in Greece. While we may think of olive wood primarily as the raw material for handsome salad bowls and accompanying utensils, it has also been used for making flutes. Spain's prime tonewood was once cypress, although poplar, boxwood, and walnut were also used in instrument making. Additional species prevalent in Spanish forests include juniper, fir, pine, alder, beech, sycamore, and a variety of others.

I asked if much Spanish wood was being used in instrument making, and Gil de Avalle replied, "The body of the flamenco guitar is made of cypress. In the past we used local cypress, but now we get it from Guadalajara," a reference to the Spanish province northeast of Madrid.

Cupressus sempervirens can live for four thousand years, and, because it grows in a spire toward the heavens, it evokes spirituality and peaceful elegance through the entire Mediterranean perimeter. "We get wood from Romania, and we have a Madagascar supplier," Gil de Avalle said. "The spruce comes from Central Europe, and Madagascar provides rosewood and ebony used for guitar backs and finger boards. Unfortunately, the guitars made with nonthreatened species don't sound the same."

Cordoba Guitars, a major manufacturer of nylon-string classical guitars located in Santa Monica, California, has based its instruments on the designs of Torres and Hauser. While steel-stringed guitars support much more tension, they are heavier than those strung with nylon, which convey delicacy and lightness—"like a kite," as one designer put it. Arched tops are carved for f-hole guitars, but flamenco and classical guitars are flat. At Cordoba, I saw a useful chart showing where on a scale between warmth and brightness various tonewoods fall. Rosewood backs and sides are on the warm side, maple and cypress are bright. Tops made of Indian rosewood and cedar are warm, while Sitka spruce is the brightest. European Norway spruce occupies the center of the scale with a balanced, even tone.

Experts point out seven major differences between the flamenco and classical guitars: wood types, weight, body thickness, sound and tone, string height, buzz, and tapping board. Taken together, all these distinctions, along with subtler ones such as bracing patterns, are in service of playing two very different kinds of music. A flamenco guitar is most often made with a spruce top and cypress sides, while a classical guitar may have either a spruce or a cedar top. A variety of woods can be used for the backs and sides of a classical guitar, but most commonly woods for this purpose are on the warm side of the tone spectrum, ideally rosewood.

The flamenco guitar, considerably lighter in weight and thinner between the top and the back, is designed for brightness and much higher volume in order to accompany loud singing and dancing. The sound of a classical guitar, conversely, is pure, resonant, and warm. Played side by side, the flamenco guitar can easily drown out the classical guitar.

The strings on a flamenco guitar are set lower to enable rapid fingering technique and a rougher buzzing sound on the frets, whereas the classical guitar strings are raised to avoid buzzing. As Ahmad Ahdab, a professional flamenco guitarist who calls himself Dr. ANTF, explains, "[Buzz] is desired in flamenco; we like it. It's a kind of technique similar

Antonio Bernal showing certified Spanish cypress used for a flamenco guitar, Seville, Spain.

to playing an electric guitar when you play a pattern and use distortion. For electric guitars, you want something to do this for you, but in flamenco we have it by default because the strings are lower and when we play fast the buzz will last only a short period of time. It will give you the effect of strength." The flamenco guitar can create a feeling of raw drama, accentuated by the golpe technique. This strong tapping on the soundboard, which is often protected with a plastic guard, heightens the excitement.

Antonio Bernal is another highly regarded Andalusian guitar luthier whose workshop, Guitarrería Alvarez & Bernal, is in Seville. His workbench, his usable tonewood stock, and the instruments for sale all fit into a single room. Black-framed photographs of famous musicians cover the walls between finished and unfinished guitars and racks of tonewood and cutouts of tops and backs. A demonstration board hung to the right shows the internal bracing structure, top and back, for a flamenco guitar and for a classical guitar. Bracing patterns for guitar tops are often the signature innovations of the greatest luthiers. Antonio de Torres created a very symmetrical support structure that resembled a pleated dress, called a fan pattern. Three spruce struts run near the upper part of the guitar, one next to the neck and two close to the sound hole. Toward the bottom the spruce bracing splays into the Torres seven, but guitar luthiers constantly experiment to create something that enhances volume and tone. Asymmetries that vary Torres's signature pattern developed as the luthier built larger guitars for volume. Even the Hora director in Romania, Bazgan, experimented with guitar bracing to enhance sound transmission.

Antonio Bernal first showed me two chocolate-colored billets with the outline for a guitar drawn in white. "This is Indian rosewood, and it will be cut for the back of a classical guitar." Then he showed me billets cut from a much lighter, blond-colored wood. "This is Spanish cypress. Cypress in Spain is at an end," he said ruefully. "Now it comes from Turkey. But *this* one is Spanish cypress, and it will have a certificate of origin. It's only for a flamenco guitar, this wood."

11

Luthiers and Alternative Sources

SINKER WOOD, FLOORBOARDS, AND BACKYARD TREES

SAYUMI TAKAHASHI HARB, A violinist, translator, and Asian studies professor, realized after years of practicing and performing that her concert-level violin might be too long for her arms and hands, leading to discomfort. The demands on the body from the repetitive motions used when playing the violin for years can cause musculoskeletal disorders affecting the jaw, back, neck, shoulder, and hands. Searching for an instrument better suited to her, she tried seven or eight top-level violins before commissioning a violin from the acclaimed New York City–based luthier Andrius Faruolo. In the process, she became very knowledgeable about tonewoods, speaking with particular appreciation of sinker wood, which she prefers to call submerged wood. This wood comes from underwater in bays, in lakes, from silt, from sunken things: piers, pilings, boats, lost logs, fish traps. Many logs also sink during floatage on the rivers used to transport them. These sunken logs have acquired surprising value, mainly to furniture makers. Takahashi Harb explained that Japanese carvers appreciated submerged wood not just for its durability, striking grain patterns, and sometimes the tannin-infused coloring but also for its metaphorical suggestions.

One need only look at Japanese prints to know that some of the most talented woodcarvers in the world come from Japan. The woodblock process involves the meticulous carving of a key block that leaves the fine outlines of an image, with up to fifteen subsequent blocks carved to fill in areas of color. It can take ten years to become an *ukiyo-e* master carver. Ingenious Japanese wood carvings are found large and small, embellishing whole temples or detailing palm-sized netsuke animals. With a poetic sensibility, Japanese carvers find metaphors, submerged or hidden meanings, in the sinker wood they carve. Takahashi Harb referred to a poem from the famous Heian Period Imperial anthology, the Kokinshû:

> The river of loose tongues:
> If from its shoals a drowned tree
> Should rise,
> What are we to do,
> Who have only just begun to meet?

Luthiers cherish this wood, particularly as a tonewood for guitars. George Youngblood of George Youngblood Guitars in Guilford, Connecticut, heavily relies on salvage wood of all sorts now that his primary focus as a luthier has shifted to restoration, and many of the necessary materials are difficult to acquire.

In college, Youngblood studied anthropology, but afterward he supported himself by making and restoring furniture. His passion for working with wood led him to lutherie, and ultimately he not only developed his own business but also became an expert consultant to Martin & Co. and Gibson. He is now one of the most sought-after repair luthiers in the United States. His workshop, showrooms, and home are all contained in a two-story colonial farmhouse that has been lifted off its foundation and moved a hundred feet back from the busy Boston Post Road. Youngblood had transformed his property, sandwiched between the cemetery and the West River marsh, into a small private arboretum. He also sells acoustic instruments out of his house, managed by a long-time associate. They offer Collings, Taylor, Bourgeois, and Santa Cruz guitars and have a selection of mandolins, banjos, and ukuleles. Youngblood is a bit of a loner and sometimes becomes impatient with star musicians that come to his shop. He joked that "it's like having adolescents in your workshop."

Youngblood surveyed a pair of billets for a guitar he was making for his son. "This wood is Sitka spruce, Native American–cut and recovered from fish traps," he told me. "It's the same type of wood that was used for totem poles. It resists weathering."

He explained that Sitka spruce forests had suffered materially from clearcutting practices, leading to a scarcity of the primary tonewood used by major guitar manufacturers such as Gibson, Martin, Yamaha, Taylor, and Fender, along with the piano makers Steinway & Sons, Baldwin, and Yamaha. Fortunately—and surprisingly, too, to the nonexpert—salvage wood cured in salty North Pacific waters could potentially be used in instrument making. Alaskan fish traps in the past were made with weighted spruce logs, which when aged in airtight submerged conditions produce prized tonewood billets. Without oxygen, the wood doesn't rot, and while sunken on river bottoms or in lakes and estuaries, minerals replace sap, making the wood even stiffer and better for tonewood. Youngblood explained that sinker wood of other tree species also acquires attractive hues for backs and sides on guitars and mandolins. Besides Sitka spruce, sunken cedar and redwood logs prized by North American luthiers are salvaged and milled for instrument making. In the Carolinas, cypress logs sunken for more than a century can be worth up to $7,000, primarily to furniture makers. Sinker wood divers now scour river bottoms like treasure hunters, which indeed they are.

In the eighteenth and nineteenth centuries, log floating practices damaged riverbanks: as cover was removed, erosion followed, and the beds themselves were disturbed by channeling, debris, and explosives used on logjams. Even splash dams were constructed to accumulate water and then release it to drive logs. Today, with the hunting of sunken wood, the problem of disturbing the rivers reemerges. Extensive sinker wood salvage disrupts delicate ecological balances, in particular adversely affecting wild trout and salmon spawning. The sunken logs provide a welcoming habitat over time by changing the river flow and creating gravel beds where young fish can hatch and be protected from strong currents as they develop. Rivers are becoming legally protected from log salvagers, who also face such impediments as gaining permission to work on private or protected nature reserve lands.

Youngblood made it clear how resourceful and imaginative luthiers must be, particularly in instrument restoration. Holding a newly braced soundboard, Youngblood said, "I'm not an instrument-maker anymore. I'm primarily a restorer. This piece will replace a smashed top on a fifty-year-old Martin guitar." He picked up a rectangular strip of black wood. "This fingerboard will also be a replacement. And this is the neck I made. Not much left to this woman's guitar, really." Some materials for restoration can be difficult to find, and many of the original parts are now illegal to acquire: Gabon ebony, Brazilian rosewood, hawksbill tortoise shell, white abalone, ivory.

Luthiers like Youngblood are always on the hunt for materials. "I have carcasses in the basement," he said cheerfully. "There's a whole pile of broken guitars I call 'organ donors.' The pressure is on for these materials, not so much with the repairman as with the builder. The repairmen can find a way to get the materials, like these, for example. I ripped these pieces on a table saw. The wood is perfectly quarter-sawn, tight-grained white spruce, and comes from the wing braces on a World War I–era biplane. The plane was being restored, and the guy who was associated with the work recovered wooden parts, including these."

Youngblood's job for decades had been diagnosing what works and what does not work acoustically, identifying flaws and mistakes in the physical entity of an instrument that affect its musicality. The process engages all the senses. He can look at a piece of wood like the airplane brace and sense its musical value. "Yeah. This is beautiful air-dried, aged wood with a story." This was also Youngblood's passion as a luthier, the anthropologist in him. He was drawn to materials not just with sound resonance but also with an additional human legacy.

Youngblood is a savior of forsaken guitars, banjos, and mandolins. "I can't look at that 1920 mandolin without thinking of the mandolin orchestras of 1920. Bluegrass wasn't invented for another twenty years." An ornate, sunburst Gibson F4 mandolin with body and head scrolls lay on his carpeted bench.

He picked up another instrument and added, "Sometimes I just want to know how come, for instance, this Gibson L7 has bird's-eye maple and a curly maple neck when all the other L7s were just plain maple." The light, honey-colored archtop glowed in his hands. Over the years, Youngblood had been hired as a consultant, most notably training Martin & Co. luthiers in restoration techniques.

Youngblood showed me the small arboretum he had planted on the edge of the West River tidal marsh. In the autumn sun, he pointed out the tree species used for tonewood: red and white spruce, maple, alder, cedar, and even wisteria, which is used in fiddle bows. His collection of trees—living versions of the cured materials in his workshop—appeared to give him deep pleasure.

Youngblood is a raconteur, and among his many stories was one concerning Gibson's legal problems. Federal marshals had raided Gibson factories in 2009 and 2011, citing violations of the Lacey Act, a wildlife conservation law originally enacted in 1900 to prevent the harvesting of game birds in one state for the purpose of sale in another. The law aimed also to thwart the introduction of non-native and exotic animal species into American ecosystems. In 2008 the Lacey Act was expanded to include broader antitrafficking protections for endangered wildlife and plants. The law now requires legal certification for users of products of protected plants, enabling officials to trace them to the original source. Gibson—accused of trafficking in endangered species, specifically the slow-growing Madagascar ebony—bitterly contested the charges, but ultimately paid a hefty fine plus legal fees.

The large guitar companies are suffering. C. F. Martin & Co., for example, used Brazilian rosewood in numerous models of acoustic guitars, some played by top recording artists, and complained that their logistics staff spent 40 percent of its time complying with the new regulatory demands. Some instrument companies argue that they require very small amounts of wood from endangered species for guitars, clarinets, and oboes, and some feel they are being unjustly penalized because large industries, such as luxury furniture makers, smuggle rosewood. With sharp international restrictions on the use of endangered woods that give high-end instruments their unmatchable sound, the major guitar makers have found their exports dropping by as much as 30 percent.

Climate change is playing its part as well. It has been suggested that the trees used for the golden age Cremona instruments may have grown during a mini-Ice Age that contributed to slow growth, and thus tight tree rings. We are now living in an age of increasing heat and drought, which severely afflict Norway spruce, and violent storms that level forests just as efficiently as decades of clearcutting. Stringed-instrument making represents a minuscule percentage of wood exploitation, and perhaps by comparison with the use of wood for parquet flooring and furniture making, Martin and Gibson feel victimized by regulations. Should they be exempt? The pressure on their market comes from stiff international competition, foremost from Asia. Indeed, forest management for exotic woods is undeveloped in many tropical countries, and now rampant fires, attributed to global warming, vandalism, and corrupt farming practices are taking a toll that will likely increase and will be hard to assess.

Whether it is a salmon river with sinker wood being extracted, clearcutting in the Balkans or Alaska, or exploitation of resources in

Madagascar and Brazil, the environment changes, and nature reacts in return. At the millennium, 7,000 trees at Versailles blew down, along with 60,000 in the Paris area and 5 percent overall throughout France. If any significant change is made to a specific environment—either by humans or by natural forces—equilibrium is upset, the consequences of which cannot be predicted. Some precious wood is simply salvaged after a storm, as in the Paneveggio forest, or fallen exotic trees might be harvested.

Perhaps the most famous example of salvaged wood involved a mahogany tree that attained mythic status and was dubbed "The Tree." In 1965, loggers chopped down a massive five-hundred-year-old tree in the Honduran Chiquibul rain forest that was over one hundred feet tall and ten feet in diameter. After the foresters took weeks felling the tree, it toppled capriciously in the wrong direction, landing in a ravine, making it inaccessible. A decade passed before the expert exotic wood exporter Robert Novak recognized the tree's value and had it cut in quarters for extraction. The mahogany had highly valued "tortoise shell" figuring with rich brown and caramel hues and outstanding tonal qualities. Some of the most renowned guitar makers used billets from "The Tree," producing some of the most coveted guitars. Luthier Reuben Forsland made one for Rock Hall of Fame guitarist Slash, who was literally humbled by his new instrument. "I was amazed that you can actually make a guitar that's perfect—perfect intonation, perfect tension on the neck, perfect sound."

While intelligent forest management will be necessary for supplying large-scale instrument making, small-scale individual luthiers can sometimes benefit by thinking in more resourceful, imaginative ways. Writer and filmmaker Laurie Gwen Shapiro recently revived interest in the violin maker Samuel Stochek, who recovered wood—often floorboards made of figured maple—from nineteenth-century buildings that were being demolished during the Great Depression years. Stochek's is a mercurial story of multicultural New York. He was a Jewish car mechanic hired by Ukrainian mandolin makers, who taught him their craft. Once Stochek went into the luthier business for himself, he found himself short of supplies. Lacking the financial resources to acquire tonewood stock from European suppliers, he cleverly explored the possibility of recovering suitably aged wood from gutted New York City buildings. Becoming obsessed with neighborhood demolition projects and receiving tips from his friends, he salvaged his wood from Manhattan houses, apartment buildings, the Hotel Shelburne, and Brooklyn seaboard hotels, among other places. Some of the wood in flooring or paneling had been cured for fifty or more years. He began carving salvage-wood violins. During World War II, Stochek achieved recognition and the appreciation of serious musicians for his violins.

Master luthier, tonewood expert, and instrument-making instructor Pascal Cranga takes the environment-friendly instrument to another level: instruments made from local tonewood. Cranga's training center, L'Esprit du bois, teaches professionals and amateurs both basic and advanced techniques for the creation and restoration of a large variety of stringed instruments. The center is located in Cluny, a historic town in southern Burgundy. Cluny is known for the remains of an enormous Benedictine abbey that was once of wide-ranging influence, sending monks to establish monasteries in places like Rougemont, Switzerland, below the Arses forest. The abbey was closely associated with the Old Regime and was therefore targeted. After the French Revolution and during Napoléon's First Empire, the abbey fell into disuse, and its grounds were converted into a quarry. Only one of the original eight towers now remains. Just around the corner from the abbey's ruins, on the rue du Merle, Pascal Cranga acquired space for his workshop in Maison des Vendanges, a building that formerly served as a processing center for the Burgundian wine-grape harvest.

Cranga is a distinctive-looking man. With his goatee and visored workman's beret, he has the trademark look of the master of hand-crafts. The Cranga office features four certificates honoring him and

Pascal Cranga, master luthier, tonewood expert, and teacher, in his workshop in Cluny, France.

L'Esprit du bois: two from the French Republic for an "Entreprise du patrimoine vivant" (A Living Heritage Establishment), another naming Cranga a master artisan, and the last a regional prize recognizing his contributions to his métier. When I expressed admiration, he joked that he could have printed the certificates himself since no monetary award came with the honors. The room also contained a scanner for printing plans for instruments, large or small. In contrast to Mirecourt and other formal instrument-making schools with stiff entrance requirements, L'Esprit du bois is dedicated to teaching the art of lutherie and restoration to almost anyone with a deep interest. The main workroom, with musical instruments of all sorts hanging from the ceiling, can accommodate six students at a time. Here international professionals and amateurs work side-by-side or across from one another on a range of stringed instruments. No one walks away with a degree, but everyone has the opportunity to acquire the basic knowledge necessary to create or restore an instrument. Cranga oversees and advises work not only on violins, cellos, and guitars but also on ouds, ukuleles, mandolins, and many other stringed instruments. In addition, he maintains a stock of outstanding aged tonewood that was cut in France.

The conference room at L'Esprit du bois is filled with a collection of wood samples and charts, several instruments under restoration, and a line of three ornate hurdy-gurdies. Among his many talents, Cranga is a hurdy-gurdy expert and player. The folk instrument, whose name is onomatopoeic, has a drone, sometimes a buzz from the bridge, and keys that press on the strings to make notes. It sounds like a cross between bagpipes and a violin. The hurdy-gurdy is sometimes called a wheel fiddle or a wheel lyre since a hand-cranked, rosined wooden wheel functions as a bow.

Once Cranga began discussing his craft, three key points emerged: his dedication to preserving knowledge of handcraft arts that are rapidly being lost, his embrace of an open educational model that has been unusual in France until recently, and an approach to the ecology of instrument making that parallels that of the locavore movement. In other words, use tonewood from the backyard rather than seeking exotic wood, even endangered species, from faraway lands.

He said, "I have a passion for the forest. I grew up close to the Jura, and as a child I observed and was fascinated by work in the forests and with wood. I had the luck to see in the local shops many woodworkers with fantastic skills. With one or two exceptions, they have all disappeared. In France, the work is no longer appreciated. Young people want office jobs. They don't want to become apprentices, to try again, again, and again to master the work. It's too much. They don't want to work with their hands."

Of course, he sympathized. People need to make a living, he acknowledged, to support families. Nevertheless, he remarked, "It's too bad. Many traditional skills have disappeared in the same way. What upsets me the most is that I knew gifted artisans in the Jura who could not read or write and died with their secrets, whether their medium was wood or slate. And we are now incapable of making the same things." The connection with the Cremona instruments came to mind, but also the muscle memory that great musicians have. How do you find lost secrets when they are contained in mortal bodies?

"We are not trying to find thousands of artisans," he continued, "just a few who still have secrets and gifts to pass down. In Japan, they have a real living heritage. Every century they take the temples apart and restore them anew. The knowledge and techniques are carefully preserved."

In terms of tonewood for musical instruments, Cranga reiterated the necessity for cutting wood in deep winter, but with an added point concerning insects. "The wood should have the minimum amount of sap possible. Insects attack the internal bark because it is very soft and it has sap." He pointed at the beams above in his house. "These beams are over a hundred years old. In parts they still have the inner bark but the rest of the wood is free of insects, and so hard that you can't put a knife into it. What I find fantastic is that the people who constructed this house couldn't read or write, but they had a keen sense of observation, and the wood was not cut haphazardly. Even the old firewood cutters knew to cut just before Christmas, and with the waning moon, so they would end up with less sap and fewer insects."

He showed me two billets, aged forty years, that displayed no evidence of insect damage. These had been cut just before Christmas and with the waning moon, he assured me. He tapped on the billets, confirming the wood's remarkable resonance. "Cutting wood properly is becoming more and more difficult with climate change. We no longer have a real winter, and there is a constant small movement of sap."

Turning to the topic of sinker wood, Cranga explained, "The quality of wood is completely changed when it has spent time in water. People talk about Stradivari's varnishes and other things, but what they completely forget is that there were no trucks to transport logs. Instead they put the logs in the river, and they floated down from the mountains. When wood has been in water, it is completely changed, and it doesn't have to stay submerged long."

He discussed in detail his collection of wood samples, and then brought out a selection of instruments. Among these was a guitar made nearly entirely of Tahitian koa, a spectacular and highly figured variety of acacia. "This is not an instrument from the garden. You must search far away to find the tonewood for it. It's beautiful, but it is not an instrument with good sound. You know, people often buy instruments because of their aesthetics and not for their voices. Many of the exotic woods only add an aesthetic value and not an acoustical one."

Reinforcing his argument for local wood, Cranga continued, "I am passionate about wood, but I never buy it from the Eastern European countries, even though my background is Romanian. One of the questions I have is about radioactivity. No one talks about it, but it has also become a problem with wine because of the barrels. France is the largest producer of oak barrels. The superb oak, also used for ships, comes from the Tronçais forest south of Orleans in the center of France. But there isn't enough French oak, so it was being imported from the Eastern European countries—Romania, Poland, Russia. This wood has astonishingly high levels of radiation. Soon wine barrels had to be certified that the oak comes from France." The source of the radiation was Chernobyl, site of the 1986 nuclear disaster, and Eastern Europeans know well that a number of species of fish, game, and wild mushrooms continue to show radiation levels high enough to prohibit consumption.

Here was the crux of The Spirit of Wood's approach: tonewood should come from your backyard, so to speak, to be responsible ecologically, to preserve endangered species, and to produce a very good instrument that may not look exotic but will have a strong voice.

Cranga has an optimistic, philosophical spirit that became infectious. "People worry about the tent worms destroying the foliage. I don't. A couple of years ago you couldn't go out; the worms stripped all the trees and droppings covered everything. Moths flew like a blizzard. The next year all the leaves came back. Nature has extraordinary regenerative powers. We just need patience, above all with wood for musical instruments. The most important part of making the best stringed instruments comes at the very beginning, in choosing the right trees and nurturing them while assuring the health of the forest, cutting them at the right moment, and then treating and aging the wood. It's all about patience."

Tree Rings and Beyond

A CODA

WHEN YOU VISIT THE Welcome Center at the Paneveggio violin forest in southern Tyrol, you receive a strong reminder of how trees record time. The cross section of a varnished spruce trunk is displayed with an arrow pointing to a growth ring near the center dated 1775—the American War of Independence. The next arrow close by shows the 1789 ring formed during the year of the French Revolution, and, counting outwardly to 1803, a ring marks the end of ecclesiastical control of Trentino, effectively transforming the governance of Northern Italy. The 1814 ring marks the year that the Congress of Vienna was held to negotiate relations in Europe after Napoléon's defeat. We get to Italy's first war of independence in 1848, and then several other key historical dates indicated in the tree's rings, including the years when the two world wars started in the first half of the twentieth century. The very outer ring, of course, commemorates the full year before woodcutters felled the tree.

This specimen was a healthy sapling when rebellious colonists in America would illicitly meet and plan their insurrections under designated trees that communities later celebrated as Liberty Trees.

This was the period when Thomas Jefferson served as the principal author of the Declaration of Independence. Historians point out that Jefferson was a keen music lover and avid amateur violinist. Music was a passion he shared with his wife, Martha, during their courtship and ten years of marriage. He bought her a pianoforte made in London, and would later purchase Kirkman harpsichords for his two daughters, famously saying that music would be "a companion which will sweeten many hours of life to you." His message was similar for the new country as he wished to promote greater musical sophistication for the former colonies.

Jefferson owned at least three violins, one of which was reputed to be a creation of Nicolò Amati's workshop. After Jefferson's death, the Cremona violin was apparently evaluated and sent to England for auction, and little more is known of it. He also used a newly designed bow based on innovations of François Xavier Tourte that dramatically increased the sound range a violinist could extract from the instrument. The bow was longer than the ones played on the original Amati, Stradivarius, and Guarneri instruments. Instead of arching outward over the stretched horse hairs that vibrate the strings, it curved elegantly inward and was made of a light, flexible Pernambuco instead of the snakewood, chinawood, or ironwood often used for earlier bows. Tourte, the resourceful former clockmaker, recovered Pernambuco staves from Brazilian sugar casks. With the new Tourte bow, violinists achieved increased sustain, force, and agility. Prices for a Tourte bow these days approach the same level as many of the top Cremona instruments.

Jefferson played on gut strings, but he lived long enough to see the G string become more commonly wrapped with silver or copper, a method known as half-wound (in French, *demi-filée*). During the 1820s, Louis Spohr, composer and violinist, developed the chinrest to help stabilize the violin for difficult fingering and powerful bowing. Beethoven died a year after Jefferson, his compositions exhibiting increased range from innovations in the piano and violin family of instruments.

Schubert, a Beethoven pallbearer, died two years after Jefferson, but in those years composed some of the most stunning works in the Western repertoire. Joseph Haydn, who died in 1806, was composing during Jefferson's years in Europe 1784 to 1789, and Jefferson attended concerts featuring Haydn's works. Mozart composed *The Marriage of Figaro* in 1786 and *Don Giovanni* in 1787. Indeed, Jefferson met Mozart briefly, intending to commission a composition as a tribute to his late wife.

It may be impossible now to find a spruce old enough in the Paneveggio forest to contain rings dating back to Stradivari's time. However, the tightest grain in the bellies of some of his violins, violas, and cellos would date to a time when music began to shift from the monophonic melodies of plainsong and Gregorian chants to early Renaissance harmony and polyphony with multiple melody lines. Compositional complexity would evolve along the entire spectrum of forms, from songs and chants for a single voice to string quartets. To go back through tree rings to the oldest surviving stringed instruments, the lyres of Ur, dating to around 2500 BCE, one would need a bristlecone pine, a twisted, tortured-looking tree not used for tonewood but the subject of a country song written by Hugh Prestwood. The chronicle of bristlecone tree rings would include the Greek philosopher Theophrastus, who, during the third century BCE, observed that wood is composed of many layers throughout, "like an onion." Leonardo da Vinci understood, nearly two millennia later, that the thickness of the annual layers of growth varied with the amount of precipitation in a given year. However, it took the pioneering astronomer A. E. Douglass, studying the occurrence of droughts with varying sun activity, to discover the effects of weather changes recorded in very old ponderosa pines. Douglass established dendrochronology, a science in which arboreal "life experiences" are mapped on a tree's rings as a way of understanding both human history and the health of the planet.

What will the tree rings reveal about our times and the future of tonewood and lutherie? A. E. Douglass surely detected in trees the mini-Ice Age that other scientists have found recorded in the wood of

Cremona stringed instruments. Future studies will see in certain tree rings evidence of the fires, droughts, and storms that have marked climate change in the twenty-first century. The painful irony is that many of the devastated forests contain protected, endangered trees, making them all the more vulnerable in the future. With the ever-increasing difficulty of acquiring top-notch traditional tonewood, many luthiers and factories are trying alternative woods, especially for ebony, all true rosewoods, select mahoganies, Pernambuco, and numerous others on the CITES "red list."

Instrument makers are also looking for inexpensive, low-maintenance, durable materials that can speed up the process of producing instruments while competing admirably with the acoustical qualities that wood provides. Carbon fiber, also known as graphite fiber, is a relatively new addition to manufacturing that we have come to recognize as a high-performance material: light, rigid, and resilient. It is used for racing bikes, golf clubs, boats, airliners, bridges, and even NASA space vehicles. Carbon fiber is made of very thin carbon crystals formed into filaments called by some "black silk." These filaments are woven together to produce one of our strongest construction materials when made into a composite with resin. For years, carbon fiber composite has been used for lightweight protective instrument cases. Recently, carbon fiber bows have become highly appreciated alternatives to the imperiled Pernambuco, the brazilwood prized in traditional archéterie. Serious luthiers would cringe seeing poorly made bows or ones for children using precious Pernambuco. Carbon fiber offers an excellent alternative, and pricy top-of-the-line bows have been crafted from this material for professionals.

Now adventurous musical instrument makers have embraced carbon fiber technology. They have started to use carbon fiber to construct the violin family of instruments, harps, flutes, mandolins, parts of brass instruments, and pianos. Of course, as the quality of carbon fiber acoustic instruments improves, the debate intensifies over whether to purchase a carbon fiber or a wood violin or cello. The makers of carbon fiber instruments tout the warmth and projection of their instruments, their reliability, particularly in outdoor concerts or unusual concert hall conditions, and their maintenance, which entails a mere wipedown with a little Windex. They publish the endorsements of professional musicians, including Yo-Yo Ma, who has used his Luis and Clark composite cello when performing outdoors in temperatures that exceed 100 degrees.

Guitar luthiers and manufacturers are the most intrepid inventors. Ovation Guitars produced a fiberglass round body guitar in 1966 and then patented the first carbon fiber tops in 1974. Blackbird Guitars in San Francisco made a reputation looking at composite materials for their instruments, working with carbon fiber and also from what they call "Ekoa," a biocomposite made using fibers from the flax plant, the source of linen. Blackbird markets wood-free, worry-free instruments it characterizes as "part mountain dulcimer and part F1 race car."

For the composite-material instruments, a mold is created, and resin-treated carbon fiber or flax fiber woven fabric is layered before the mold is vacuum sealed. Some instruments are molded in one piece, neck and body. Handwork is required in cutting and burnishing rough edges and rigging the instrument with fingerboard, tuners, strings, and chinrest.

Some luthiers will undoubtedly take advantage of such technologies as computer numerical control (CNC) of milling machines. These small programmable router machines can relieve luthiers of the tedious roughing-out process from wood blocks and billets. Along these lines, electronic tools that calibrate thicknesses of wood and can test resonance will aid luthiers in the creation of great instruments. Scientific analysis of masterpiece instruments will continue to provide intelligence to luthiers in their production of new instruments of arguably similar quality. The use of technology has led to the emergence of what is known as digital instrument craft. This expression refers to both electronic music inventions and traditional stringed instruments carved using lasers and computers. Digital luthiers develop instrument designs incorporating acoustical data and program interfaces on their computers that guide CNC routing and milling machines. Finishing work and fine adjustments will still be completed traditionally, by hand.

In 1989, Bob Taylor was one of the first in North America to use CNC machines for crafting Taylor acoustic guitars. At the time, artisans considered robotic milling in lutherie practically a sin, removing the hard-earned knowledge and selective instincts from instrument making. In the ensuing years, Taylor guitars greatly profited, for buyers could still enjoy excellent instruments while paying lower prices. Now individual luthiers can acquire versions of these CNC machines.

Given the competition of factories, the increasing difficulty of accessing outstanding tonewood, and the legal restrictions on exotic woods, one can easily imagine luthiers and specialized tonewood millers being pessimistic about the future of their specialties. Even changes in musical tastes could alter their prospects. But from my experience talking to luthiers and tonewood experts, the outlook seems generally upbeat. No one I interviewed is getting rich from their work. Optimism in the world of stringed instrument making is based on several trends, one of which I heard mentioned repeatedly: the open sharing of ideas and experience among luthiers and tonewood sellers. This sharing occurs during workshops, at international musical instrument festivals, and in online forums. Most important, the optimism is based on a long tradition of and love for crafting wood into extraordinary objects with voices. A master luthier will have spent ten years as an apprentice to acquire instrument-making skills and develop a sensibility for selecting the best wood and how each billet should be carved to produce the best possible voice. Luthiers are comparable to the master Japanese carpenters who train and apprentice for renovating temples originally made without nails more than a millennium ago. Both are traditional craft arts.

The historical timeline for the emergence of dendrology often includes a passage from Montaigne's Italian travel diary describing his encounter with a carpenter:

> The man who made these wares, an artist of great talent and famous as a maker of fine mathematical instruments, informed me, that all trees, when cut through, show as many rings as they have years, and he gave me demonstration of this from all the different sorts of wood he had in his shop, he being a carpenter. The part of the tree which faces the north is always of closer grain and with circles nearer together than the other parts. Wherefore, he boasts that, whatever specimen of wood may be brought to him, he can always determine how old was the tree from which it was cut, and the aspect towards which it faced.

The point, from a scientific perspective, is that carpenters and wood carvers, often sculpting for churches, understood that the life of a tree was recorded in its grain. The wisdom was passed down orally over centuries and reinforced by the observations and experiences of artisans.

It would be hard to imagine Thoreau, a music lover and skeptical about technology, being thrilled with playing a carbon composite flute. The flute he inherited from his brother and played at Walden Pond was made of boxwood. It had a romantic spirit of its own—one that Louisa May Alcott captured in her elegy "Thoreau's Flute." Thoreau himself might well have said that the very pores of the boxwood rejoiced in music. He particularly enjoyed playing on Walden Pond for the echo it produced. "In warm evenings," he wrote, "I frequently sat in the boat playing the flute, and saw the perch, which I seemed to have charmed, hovering around me, and the moon travelling over the ribbed bottom, which was strewed with the wrecks of the forest."

While boxwood is traditionally appreciated for baroque flutes and recorders, musicians and instrument makers might argue the merits of other flute tonewoods. Flutes have a history going back to bird bones and reeds. The optimistic spirit of today's luthiers is inspiring because they, with all their skill, know their craft is based on two essential things: the variability and musical potential of wood, and their own human sensibility, their personal taste. In a future timeline, we will still find synergies of passion among forest managers, tonewood millers, inspired luthiers, musicians, and composers—all of them looking for a special voice, and a larger palate of sound.

ACKNOWLEDGMENTS

This book is in large part based on many encounters and discussions with forestry experts, instrument makers, tonewood suppliers, and musicians. They took time out of their busy schedules and welcomed me into their homes, workshops, or factories to share their experiences and wisdom about tonewood and forests. I am indebted to Antoine Cauche, Henri Alécian, Bernard Michaud, Mihai Filip, Sayumi Takahashi Harb, George Youngblood, Pascal Cranga, Nicolae Bazgan, Jan Bobak, Maciek Bobak, Grzegorz Bobak, Andrea Frandsen, Sarah Hammel Gueta, Dr. Reinhard Zach, Jousson Robin, Jean-Pierre Neff, Silviu Cira, Ondřej Kubart, Daniel Gil de Avalle, Antonio Bernal, and Paul Hostetter.

Each book is a long journey that is enhanced by fellow travelers, contributors, and supportive friends. I thank Laurent and Catherine Harvey for encouraging me to write this book from the beginning and sending helpful materials and to Hélène Collandre for contributing a much-needed diagram. Thank you to composer Chris Culpo and artist-writer Anne Graaff, who joined the journey. My special appreciation for the help of literary agent Laura Strachan and of my abiding friend for so many years, Susan Prospere, who helped me improve this text. Deep gratitude goes to Charles Siebert, who has set a new standard for nature writing.

I am particularly grateful to Boyd Zenner, senior acquiring editor, with whom I have worked for over a decade, and to the University of Virginia Press family, especially Emily Grandstaff, Jason Coleman, and Ellen Satrom.

I greatly appreciate the faculty development grants awarded to me by my colleagues at the American University of Paris. They helped support extensive travel.

SOURCES

Allen, Aaron S. "'Fatto di Fiemme': Stradivari's Violins and the Musical Trees of the Paneveggio." In *Invaluable Trees: Cultures of Nature, 1660–1830,* ed. Laura Auricchio, Elizabeth Heckendorn Cook, and Giulia Pacini (Oxford: SVEC, 2012), 301.

Antonio Stradivari: Violoncello Stauffer ex Cristiani. Edited by Eric Blot. Cremona: Consorzio Liutrai Antonio Stradivari Cremona, 2009, 18.

"Arkpabi Completes Stunning Renovation of the Museo del Violino in Cremona, Italy." *Interior Design,* May 14, 2017.

Ballu, Jean-Marie. *Bois de musique: La forêt berceau de l'harmonie.* Paris: Éditions du Gerfaut, 2004.

Barron, James. "Seeking the Perfect Piano Piece, in Spruce." *New York Times,* June 10, 2003.

Blumberg, George P. "From Wood and String: Crafting Sound That's Vintage." *New York Times,* July 7, 2002. (Profile of George Youngblood.)

La botanica della musica. Edited by Gabriele Rinaldi. Bergamo, Italy: Orto Botanico di Bergamo, 2007.

Bremaud, Iris. "What Do We Know on 'Resonance Wood' Properties? Selective Review and Ongoing Research." HAL, April 23, 2012, https://hal.archives -ouvertes.fr/hal-00811117/document.

Bressan, David. "The Mysterious Microbial Origins of Mountains." *Scientific American,* June 21, 2012.

Butler, Rhett. "Endangered Species Trafficking: What Did Gibson Guitar Know?" Mongabay.com, July 7, 2011, https://news.mongabay.com/2011/07/endangered -species-trafficking-what-did-gibson-guitar-know/.

Carletti, Paolo, Elena Vendramin, Diego Pizzeghello, et al. "Soil Humic Compounds and Microbial Communities in Six Spruce Forests as Function of Parent Material, Slope Aspect and Stand Age." *Plant Soil* 315 (2009): 47–65.

Castle, Danielle. "Sunken Treasure." *Made by Custommade* (blog), CustomMade .com, December 22, 2014, https://www.custommade.com/blog/underwater -timber/.

Cho, Adrian. "Million-Dollar Strads Fall to Modern Violins in Blind 'Sound Check.'" *Science,* May 9, 2017.

Cohen, Edie. "Arkpabi Completes Stunning Renovation of the Museo del Violino in Cremona, Italy." *Interior Design,* May 14, 2017, https://www.interiordesign .net/projects/12969-arkpabi-completes-stunning-renovation-of-the-museo-del -violino-in-cremona-italy/.

Cowling, Elizabeth. *The Cello.* New York: Charles Scribner's Sons, 1975.

"Cremona Musica—The Piano Experience." *David Crombie's World Piano News,* September 5, 2018.

Cumpiano, William R., and Jonathan D. Natelson. *Guitarmaking: Tradition and Technology.* San Francisco: Chronicle Books, 1993.

Dermoncourt, Bertrand. "Les mystères des Stradivarius révélés." *L'Express,* February 18, 2010.

Dico, Joy Lo. "The Rush to Rescue Harmonic Wood from Italy's 'Forest of Violins.'" *Financial Times,* December 14, 2018.

Doran, Michael. "Making Purfling." Doran Violins, December 23, 2009, http://www .doranviolins.com/workbench/making-purfling/.

Dudley, Kathryn Marie. *Guitar Makers: The Endurance of Artisanal Values in North America.* Chicago: University of Chicago Press, 2014, 119.

Easton, Carol. *Jacqueline du Pré: A Biography.* Boston: Da Capo Press, 2000, 158, 159.

Estrella, Espie. "The History of the Violin." ThoughtCo, May 2, 2018, https://www .thoughtco.com/the-history-of-the-violin-2455855.

Fanelli, Damian. "Segovia's Dream Guitar: The Master's 1937 Hermann Hauser SR." *Guitar Player,* August 21, 2013.

Fantel, Hans. "Improving the Sound of Outdoor Concerts." *New York Times,* Arts section, July 17, 1983.

Fernow, Bernhard. *A Brief History of Forestry: In Europe, the United States, and Other Countries.* Toronto: University of Toronto Press, 1907.

Finkelstein, Katherine E. "In Concert, Searchers Retrieve Yo-Yo Ma's Lost Stradivarius." *New York Times,* October 17, 1999.

Gardiner, Barry. "Trees Break at Fixed Wind Speed, Irrespective of Size or Species." PhysicsWorld, February 10, 2016. https://physicsworld.com/a/trees-break-at -fixed-wind-speed-irrespective-of-size-or-species/.

Germann, Peter, and Peter Holland. "Fragmented Ecosystems: People in the Mountains of Switzerland and New Zealand." *Mountain Research and Development* 21, no. 4 (November 2001): 383, 384.

Grissino-Mayer, Henri D., and L. H. Berkle. "Stradivari, Violins, Tree Rings, and the Maunder Minimum: A Hypothesis." *Dendrochronologia* 21, no. 1 (December 2003): 41–45.

Grissino-Mayer, Henri D., Paul R. Sheppard, and Malcolm K. Cleveland. "A Dendroarchaeological Re-examination of the 'Messiah' Violin and Other Instruments Attributed to Antonio Stradivari." *Journal of Archaeological Science* 31 (2004): 167–74.

"Guitar Makers Hit Hard by New Regulations on Prized Rosewood." Associated Press, April 12, 2018.

Harding, Walter. "A Bibliography of Thoreau in Music." *Studies in the American Renaissance,* 1992, 291–315.

Heshmat, Sharam. "Why Are We Moved by Music?" *Psychology Today,* July 24, 2018.

Hoffman, Jascha. "Q&A: Violin Detective." *Nature* 513, no. 486 (2014).

Huismans, Ritske, Giovanni Bertotti, D. Ciulavu, et al. "Structural Evolution of the Transylvanian Basin (Romania): A Sedimentary Basin in the Bend Zone of the Carpathians." *Tectonophysics* 272, no. 2 (1997): 249–68.

"The Ice City." Marmalada Grand Guerra, n.d., http://www.museomarmoladagrande guerra.com/en/the-museum/the-ice-city/.

Isacoff, Stuart. "The Violin Museum Is a Luthier's Paradise." *Wall Street Journal,* March 7, 2018.

Johnson, Art. "1720 'Red Mendelssohn' Stradivarius." Blog post, *The Devil's Violin,* September 2014, http://thedevilsviolin-artjohnson.blogspot.com/2014/09/1720 -red-mendelssohn-stradivarius.html.

Katz, Cheryl. "Small Pests, Big Problems: The Global Spread of Bark Beetles." *Yale Environment 360,* September 21, 2017, https://e360.yale.edu/features/small-pests -big-problems-the-global-spread-of-bark-beetles.

Kavanaugh, Patrick. *Music of the Great Composers: A Listener's Guide to the Best Classical Music.* Grand Rapids, MI: Zondervan Publishing House, 1996, 73.

Kemp, Mark. "The Legend of 'The Tree,' a Mythic Source of 500-Year-Old Mahogany Coveted by Slash, Andy McKee, and More." *Acoustic Guitar,* January 20, 2016.

Kjorness, Criss. "Delta Dawn: How Sears, Roebuck & Co. Midwifed the Birth of the Blues." *Reason: Free Minds and Free Markets,* May 2012.

Komara, Edward, and Peter Lee. *The Blues Encyclopedia.* New York: Routledge, 2004.

Kurat, Thomas. "Wilderness Dürrenstein," n.d., https://www.wildnisgebiet.at/en/.

Leslie, Jimmy. "The Troublesome Truth about Sitka Spruce." *Guitar Player,* May 31, 2007.

Liu, Vincent. "The Cello: An Amazing Musical Instrument." *Journal of Music and Dance* 1, January 2011.

Mairson, Harry. "Secrets of Stradivari." *Stanford Magazine,* March 2018.

Marchese, John. *The Violin Maker: A Search for the Secret of Craftsmanship, Sound, and Stradivari.* New York: Harper Perennial, 2008.

Marica, Irina. "Romanian Senate Adopts Project Allowing Deforestation in Virgin Forest Areas." Romania Insider, February 22, 2018, https://www.romania-insider .com/project-allowing-deforestation-virgin-forests/.

McKean, James N. "The Art of Purfling—and the Dangers of Making It in a Bathtub." *String Magazine,* August 15, 2016.

McLennan, J. E. "The Effect of the Soundpost on Violin Sound." Music Acoustics, Physics Department, University of New South Wales, Sydney, Australia, https:// newt.phys.unsw.edu.au/music/people/mclennan_soundpost.html.

McSmith, Andy. "Virtuoso's Trip Destroys Priceless Stradivarius." *Independent,* February 13, 2008.

Micheletti, Rick. "A Peek into Lutherie Workshops around the World: Grzegorz Bobak." *Strad,* August 2015.

Milton, John. *The Complete Poetry and Essential Prose of John Milton.* Edited by William Kerrigan, John Rumrich, and Stephen M. Fallon. New York: Modern Library, 2007.

Montaigne, Michel de. *The Journal of Montaigne's Travels in Italy: By Way of Switzerland and Germany in 1580 and 1581 Volume 3.* London: J. Murray. Kindle Edition, HardPress, 2017.

Nagyvary, Joseph. "Investigating the Secrets of the Stradivarius." Royal Society of Chemistry, UK, Education in Chemistry, July 1, 2005, https://eic.rsc.org/feature /investigating-the-secrets-of-the-stradivarius/2020139.article.

Norwich, John Julius. "Venice—the City That Created Opera." *Guardian,* September 30, 2013.

"Origin and Meaning of Guitar." *Online Etymology Dictionary,* https://www .etymonline.com/word/guitar.

Parker, Thomas. *Tasting French Terroir: The History of an Idea.* Oakland: University of California Press, 2015.

Peter, Laurence. "Romania Acts to Save Forests from Logging Spree." *BBC News,* May 21, 2015, quoting Gabriel Paun.

Powers, Wendy. "Violin Makers: Nicolò Amati (1596–1684) and Antonio Stradivari (1644–1737)." *Met,* October 2003.

Robbins, Jim. "Chronicles of the Rings: What Trees Tell Us." *New York Times,* April 30, 2019.

"The 'Sabionari' Stradivarius Guitar, 1679." *Strad,* June 13, 2018.

Sachs, Curt. "The Renaissance (1400–1600)." In *The History of Musical Instruments.* Mineola, NY: Dover Publications, 2006.

Scott, Heather K. "The Paganini Stradivaris: A One of a Kind Quartet." *Chamber Music New Zealand,* May 23, 2013.

"Seven Contemporary Makers on the Trade Today, How It Relates to the Past, and the Way Forward." *Strings Magazine,* November 14, 2016.

Shapiro, Laurie Gwen. "The Man Who Made Violins Out of New York City Buildings." *Atlas Obscura,* March 15, 2018.

Shapreau, Carla. "Lost and Found. And Lost Again?" *Los Angeles Times,* February 12, 2006.

Siderius, Christina. "Lawmakers Float Plan for Underwater Logging." *Seattle Times,* February 2, 2005.

Silverman, William Alexander. *The Violin Hunter.* London: William Reeves, 1964.

Splechtna, Bernhard E., and Karl Splechtna. "Rothschild's Wilderness." *Arcadia,* no. 4 (Spring 2016).

"Stradivari's Forests Destroyed in Storms." *Strad,* November 5, 2018.

"The Structure of Wood II." University of Cambridge, DoITPoMS, May 2006, last updated January 2008, https://www.doitpoms.ac.uk/tlplib/wood/index.php.

Taylor, Joseph E. III. *Making Salmon: An Environmental History of the Northwest Fisheries Crisis.* Seattle: University of Washington Press, 2001.

Tenenbaum, David J. "Underwater Logging: Submarine Rediscovers Lost Wood." *Environmental Health Perspectives,* November 2004.

Thiekjer, Mark G., Adam Boratyński, and Władysław Bugała. *Biology and Ecology of Norway Spruce.* Dordrecht, Netherlands: Springer, 2007.

Thompson, Ken. "Do Conifers Make Soil More Acid?" *Telegraph,* February 15, 2014.

Thoreau, Henry D. *Walden.* New York: Signet; Reissue edition, 2012.

———. *The Writings of Henry David Thoreau: Journal III September 16, 1851–April 30, 1852.* Boston: Houghton Mifflin, 1906.

Tissot, Tatiana. "Swiss Folk Music: 5 Traditional Instruments." Federal Department of Foreign Affairs, House of Switzerland, last updated April 26, 2019, https://houseofswitzerland.org/swissstories/society/swiss-folk-music-5-traditional-instruments.

Tudge, Colin. *The Tree: A Natural History of What Trees Are, How They Live, and Why They Matter.* New York: Crown Publishers, 2007.

Van Gelderen, D. M., P. C. de Jong, and H. J. Oterdom. *Maples of the World.* Portland, OR: Timber Press, 1994.

"Violin History." Vienna Symphonic Library, 2002, https://www.vsl.co.at/en/Violin/History/.

Winternitz, Emanuel. "The School of Gaudenzio Ferrari and the Violin." In *The Commonwealth of Music,* ed. Gustave Reese and Rose Bandel. New York: Free Press, 1965.

Wohlleben, Peter. *The Hidden Life of Trees.* Translated by Jane Billinghurst. London: William Collins, 2016.

Wyeth, Leonard. "The Lacey Act." AcousticMusic.org, 2010, https://acousticmusic.org/research/environment-government/the-lacey-act/.

Zucchino, David. "1800s-Era Sunken Logs Are Now Treasure; Here Are the Men Who Find Them." *Los Angeles Times,* July 13, 2014.

Zücher, Ernst. "Plants and the Moon: Traditions and Phenomena." American Botanical Council, *HerbalEGram* 8, no. 4 (April 2011), https://soin-de-la-terre.org/wp-content/uploads/PlantsandtheMoon.pdf.

INDEX

European Union, 111, 132
exotic wood, 41, 112, 155, 156, 159, 161, 168

Fabricatore, Gennero, 138
Faruolo, Andrius, 150
favola d'Orfeo, La, 49
Ferrari, Gaudenzio, 47, 48
Ferrer, Eduardo, 143
f-holes, 22, 24, 47, 74, 110, 123, 126, 147
fiddles, 47, 154; cigar box fiddles, 135;
    wheel fiddles, 159
figuring, 8, 12, 23, 26, 28, 45, 50, 75, 76,
    90, 98, 115, 116, 122, 137, 155, 156, 161
figuring patterns: bear claw, 23; bird's eye,
    23; crotched, 23; dimpled, 23; flamed,
    23; ghost, 23; quilted, 23; tiger, 23
Filip, Mihai, 94–102, 110, 111
fingerboard, 13, 25, 108, 109, 138, 146, 147,
    153, 167
fires, 39, 49, 54, 70, 124, 132, 155, 166
fish traps, 150, 152
flax fiber, 167
floorboards, 156; flooring, 155, 157
flotation (floatage/*flottage*), 78, 79, 103,
    150
flutes, 6, 63, 113, 146, 166, 169, 170
Fondazione Walter Stauffer, 15
foresters, 4, 6, 8, 59, 69, 83, 96, 156
forestry, 2, 35, 54, 60, 61, 73, 74, 77–79, 83,
    94, 107, 112, 114
forests, 2, 3, 6–8, 32, 35, 36, 41, 42, 45,
    52–65, 67–71, 73, 74, 76–79, 81, 82,
    87–89, 92–94, 103, 110–15, 117, 120,
    122, 123, 141, 146, 152, 155, 156, 159,
    162, 166, 171; primeval, 42, 75, 89,
    91–93, 115. *See also* Arses forest;
    Gurghiu forest; Landes forest;
    Massacre forest; Paneveggio forest;
    Risoux forest; Tronçais forest
fortepianos, 43, 50, 85–87, 104
France, 16, 17, 19–22, 33, 36, 49, 51, 54,
    57–61, 66–69, 78, 114, 121, 133, 135,
    138, 156, 158, 159, 161
Frandsen, Andrea, 18, 22, 65–67
frets, 141, 143, 147; bone frets, 141; fret
    boards, 127
fungi, 62, 67, 81, 92; *Armillaria,* 89

Gage, David, 128, 129
Gagliano, Ferdinando, 137

Garda, Lake, 31, 52
garde forestier, 61, 62
Geneva, 59, 74
Geneva, Lake, 71, 72
Gérôme, Louis, 139
Gérôme Frères, 139; Atilier Gérôme
    Frères, l', 139
Gershwin, 44
Gheogheni, 113
Gil de Avalle, Daniel, 143–46
glaciers, 39, 58, 89; glacial periods, 72
Gliga, Vasile, 103; Gliga Musical Instru-
    ment Factory, 103, 104, 127
glockenspiel, 87, 108
glue, 24, 110; hoof and hide, 25
Goffriller, Matteo, 10, 12
Gorals, 125; music, 125
Graff, Jean-Christophe, 60
grain, 2, 13–15, 22–26, 33, 34, 40, 50, 60,
    63, 64, 67, 76, 77, 79, 91, 96, 97, 108,
    123, 140, 141, 150, 153, 165, 169
Granada, 142–44
Great Depression, 127, 156
Greenpeace, 111, 114
Gregorian chants, 165
Grissino-Mayer, Henry D., 39, 40
Groblicz, Marcin, 120
ground (coating), 26
ground recipes: casein, 26; oils, 26;
    propolis, 26
ground solution of Stradivari's: calcite, 26;
    feldspar, 26; gypsum, 26; quartz, 26
groupement forestier, 74, 78
Groupement forestier du Pays-d'Enhaut
    (GFPE), 77, 78
Gstaad Dolomites, 83
Guadagnini, Geovanni Battista, 123
Guarneri family: Giuseppe, 8, 12, 17,
    31, 34, 35, 41, 46, 50, 123, 133, 164;
    Giuseppe Guarneri del Gesù (son of
    Giuseppe), 17, 30, 51
Guarnerius, 9, 29, 40
Guiliani, Mario, 138
guitar companies: Blackbird, 167; Bour-
    geois, 152; Collings, 152; Cordoba,
    147; Fender, 107, 138, 152; Gibson, 23,
    36, 107, 151, 152, 154, 155; Ibanez, 107;
    Martin, 36, 107, 108, 138, 151, 152, 153,
    154, 155; Santa Cruz, 152; Taylor, 36,
    105, 108, 152, 168